Getting into

Business & Economics Courses

Inga Morrissey

15th edition

Getting into guides

Getting into Art & Design Courses, 12th edition
Getting into Dental School, 13th edition
Getting into Engineering Courses, 7th edition
Getting into Law, 14th edition
Getting into Medical School 2024 Entry, 28th edition
Getting into Oxford & Cambridge 2024 Entry, 26th edition
Getting into Pharmacy and Pharmacology Courses, 2nd edition
Getting into Physiotherapy Courses, 11th edition
Getting into Psychology Courses, 14th edition
Getting into Veterinary School, 12th edition
How to Complete Your UCAS Application 2024 Entry, 35th edition

Getting into Business & Economics Courses
This 15th edition published in 2023 by Trotman Education, an imprint of Trotman Indigo Publishing Ltd, 21d Charles Street, Bath BA1 1HX

© Trotman Indigo Publishing Ltd 2023

Author: Inga Morrissey
14th edn: Imogen Riddick; 13th edn: Justin Edwards;
12th edn: Michael McGrath; 10th–11th edns: Carly Roberts;
8th–9th edns: James Burnett; 6th–7th edns: Kate Smith;
3rd–5th edns: Fiona Hindle; 1st–2nd edns: Trotman, published in 1994 and 1996 as *Getting into Accountancy, Business Studies and Economics*

British Library Cataloguing in Publication Data
A catalogue record for this book is available from the British Library.

ISBN 978 1 912943 80 7

Every effort has been made to trace copyright holders and to obtain their permission for the use of copyright material. The publisher apologises for any errors or omissions, and would be grateful to be notified of any corrections that should be incorporated in future editions of this book.

Printed and bound in the UK by Ashford Colour Press Ltd.

Contents

About the author

Inga Morrissey is an Assistant Principal International at Mander Portman Woodward's Cambridge college. Inga has a wealth of experience in helping UK and international students progress to highly competitive courses in business and economics, as well as supporting them with their Oxbridge applications.

Acknowledgements

I would like to thank Imogen Riddick, Justin Edwards, Michael McGrath, Carly Roberts, James Burnett, Kate Smith and Fiona Hindle, who have all written previous editions of this book, *Getting into Business & Economics Courses*. I would also like to thank Tony Marriott for his contributions to chapter 6 on current economic issues.

As far as I am aware, all information in this book is correct at the time of going to press. Unless stated otherwise, the views expressed in this book are my own.

I hope you find this guide useful and wish you every success for the future.

For up-to-date information on business, economics and related financial and management courses, please visit www.mpw.ac.uk.

Introduction

This book is entitled *Getting into Business & Economics Courses*, but also provides guidance on a wide range of courses related to management, accounting, finance and banking. The book covers all of these subjects – and more. First and foremost, this guide aims to provide information and strategies for students interested in applying to study any of the subjects listed above. The details and advice in the book are relevant to applications for courses such as accounting and finance, banking and econometrics, and for joint honours courses such as mathematics and economics.

Following a career in business, economics, management or a related area is a very popular option for graduates, and students choose courses in this sector for a variety of reasons. They gain the opportunity to develop their knowledge of management and domestic and international business by studying a range of theories, companies and organisations and by learning about and gaining practical experience of tasks such as business plans, negotiation and giving presentations. The courses are wide ranging and help students develop a number of different professional, administrative, communication and technical skills to prepare them successfully for a future job in the field. Graduates with degrees in business, economics and management can go on to such diverse careers as advertising, banking and finance, insurance and teaching.

About this book

This book is designed to give you an overview of the whole application process.

Chapter 1 looks at the types of business and economics courses available.

Chapter 2 covers work experience and the importance of internships in strengthening your application.

Chapter 3 gives advice on how to choose universities and courses and what to consider – both academically and non-academically.

Chapter 4 looks at the UCAS application and the suggested timescale for completing your application.

Chapter 5 covers the all-important personal statement and how to maximise your chances of your application being successful.

Chapter 6 details how to have a successful university interview – in terms of both preparation and how to behave in the interview itself. We also look at current economic issues and business case studies that may be useful during your interview preparation.

Chapter 7 is for anyone who is not putting forward a standard application to university; mature students as well as international students can find useful information here.

Chapter 8 looks at all of your options once you receive your results, whether they were what you wanted or not.

Chapter 9 covers fees and the types of funding you may be eligible for.

Chapter 10 discusses some of the career areas that you might think about applying to once you have graduated. This chapter goes into detail about making the first steps in your career and the options open to business and economics graduates.

Chapter 11 details where you can find further information. At the back of the book you will find a glossary of terms relating to business, economics and university admission.

This book is not meant to be a reference manual in which you look up a particular point in the contents page and go to that section: rather, it is meant to be read from the beginning to give you a complete overview of the subject, preferably well in advance of your application.

Throughout the book, the examples that quote university entrance requirements use A level grades. However, the advice is applicable to students studying Scottish Highers, the International Baccalaureate, Pre-University (Pre-U) and other qualifications. The UCAS website (www.ucas.com) lists entrance requirements for all of the major examination systems in its 'Course Search' section. If you are unsure about what you need to achieve, individual universities will be happy to give you advice; contact details are given on all of their websites.

In essence, if you are considering working in this field, this guide is designed to help you explore the entry routes and options in higher education to start you on your career.

What do businesses do?

In its widest sense, a business is an organisation that exists to fulfil the purpose decided by its owners. This definition shows us just how varied and different businesses can be. Usually, a business has to make a surplus on its trading (a profit) to be able to continue into the following year, but not all business owners see the profit motive as the single most important factor. Firms in leisure and tourism, the music industry or the media are examples of businesses that are driven by the passions of those involved. Yes, some are also highly successful financially, but it might be wrong to say that money was the sole driving force.

Even those firms that might be regarded as more mainstream are increasingly aware of the image that they present to the general public and feel that this has to be taken into consideration alongside profits. With customers and employees more discerning than ever about the ethical and sustainable practices of businesses, corporate social responsibility (CSR) is of increasing importance.

Businesses also vary greatly in their size: some are small, family-run concerns, others are vast public corporations. Many multinationals are much larger than some countries. Of the top 100 entities in the world in terms of annual turnover, about half are multinationals and the other half are countries. Working for such large organisations will obviously feel completely different from working for small- to medium-sized enterprises (SMEs) employing fewer than 250 people.

Whatever the size of the business, there are many differing approaches to running it in the best way. Business managers fulfil a variety of tasks and need a whole range of different skills. They need to inspire and give leadership, research, analyse and present information, think laterally to come up with imaginative answers, communicate with many different types of people, organise their own time and work to tight deadlines, design complex business strategies, solve conundrums and trade one interest off against another. Jobs in business are never dull because the business world is constantly changing; firms are always up against their competitors, on the one hand, and changing consumer habits, on the other. Even very big firms are not immune to failure and decline.

The way a business is run in practice is referred to as the corporate culture. This includes all of those many things that give the company its character. There are a number of different philosophies on best business practice and a variety of so-called business gurus write books and run seminars about their ideas. Tom Peters, Peter Drucker and Charles Handy are some of the more famous gurus, but there are also more obscure approaches such as *Our Iceberg is Melting: Changing and Succeeding Under Any Conditions* or *Winnie-the-Pooh on Management*. Cartoons such as Dilbert point out just how often managers get it wrong and how frustrating this is for their subordinates.

What do economists do?

Economics is the study of how individuals and groups make choices in a world where their needs and desires outweigh the availability of resources. Economics is a social science relating to every aspect of our lives, from the choices we make as individuals to the decisions made by governments across the globe. It's important to emphasise that economics is not just statistics, definitions and diagrams, as is sometimes assumed; this discipline actually helps us to frame our ideas about some of the most difficult and complex questions. Why are some countries rich and others poor? The 2022 Poverty and Shared Prosperity Report estimates that by 2030 nearly 7% of the world's population (600 million people) will be in extreme poverty. Why is global inequality still trending downward, and how has the recent pandemic exacerbated this? Why do nearly 4 billion people, or half of our global population, live on less than US$6.85 a day, as the World Bank Group estimates? People who are curious about the vast differences we see in this world often gravitate towards economics.

Economics graduates may find jobs in banking, insurance or tax, as well as with governments and large organisations such as the Bank of England. Some become academic or professional economists who develop economic theories; others manage money for wealthy individuals, investment banks or governments. Some economics graduates follow careers in accountancy or management. Others work in the transport, manufacturing, communications, insurance or retail industries. Employers value students who have studied economics because they have well-developed analytical and critical-thinking skills and are good at problem solving. Economists learn to make decisions and come to conclusions based on the analysis of numerical evidence: what are called economic indicators. Economic indicators include things such as unemployment figures, exchange rates, share prices, inflation rates and gross domestic product (GDP).

Economists use these indicators to assess whether markets or economies are likely to improve or worsen, and then to act accordingly. This could be on a small scale – deciding whether it is sensible for a company to invest in building a new factory in another country – or on a much larger scale – should a government raise or lower interest rates to try to influence the inflation rate.

Economics can be split into two broad areas: microeconomics and macroeconomics. Microeconomics looks at the behaviour of markets and consumers, including how businesses price their goods and consumer spending habits (such as why they buy a more expensive brand of washing-up liquid when a cheaper one is available). It also looks at the small-scale decisions that affect our daily lives. If petrol prices rise, should you get rid of your car? Are higher wages an incentive to work harder or to work for fewer hours? It analyses different markets, from monopolies and oligopolies to situations where there is proper competition between suppliers. Macroeconomics, on the other hand, is the study of economies as a whole, and looks at issues that have an impact on a country's financial situation; for example, inflation, balance of payments, exchange rates and the relationships between these. Macroeconomic issues are often the main headlines on the news or in your paper.

What do accountants do?

There are many different types of accountant, but one thing they have in common is that they analyse financial data and present it in a form that allows interested parties to understand what is happening in a company or business. This will enable decision makers to make an informed decision based upon all the available financial data. Also, accountants provide reports which assess the overall condition of a company. This task can be particularly important during mergers and acquisitions; decision makers need to know what they are buying if they choose to purchase a business. It is rarely the task of accountants to offer advice, but they can clearly identify areas of concern for potential purchasers of businesses, or alert existing managers to problems within a company.

Management accountants analyse budgets, sales and costs to allow the bosses to assess the past, present or future success of the business. Another type of accountant is the auditor, whose role is to check that the financial statements report true and accurate information, and that money is not being wasted or mismanaged. For a more complete picture, look at the Chartered Institute of Management Accountants' website (www.cimaglobal.com).

What do managers do?

Well, they manage things – people, organisations, communication paths, the goods or services that a business sells, and many other things besides. More about different management roles and responsibilities can be found on the Chartered Management Institute's website (www.managers.org.uk). Management is essentially the art of making things happen through people. The word 'manager' is used in almost every walk of life, from sport to banks, from shops to IT. Managers are also referred to as supervisors, project leaders and heads of departments. Managers utilise a range of skills, but primarily they need the ability to organise people and processes, to communicate or motivate effectively, and to relay the company's aims to the people underneath them in its hierarchy. Managers set objectives for those they manage, and ensure the objectives are realistic by providing the resources (financial, time, skills, personnel) to achieve those objectives. Managers also need to assess the relative success or failure of projects both during and after the lifetime of the project. Some projects may be massive (building an Olympic village) and some may be fairly small (preparing a 60-page report to be sent to a dozen colleagues for a meeting at the end of the week) but they all exhibit common challenges and common methods for improving your chances of a successful outcome.

Where to start

Once you have thought about possible areas of study or your future career options, your next stage is to do some first-hand research. This means talking to people who have experience of studying and working in these fields. A good starting point is looking at university websites, as these will often include case histories of current students and gradu-ates. Some universities offer a 'contact a student' option, so you can discuss what it is like to study one of these courses with a current student. You should also talk to careers advisers and people who are working in businesses or as economists or accountants. Getting work experience in a field you think might be for you is invaluable. Not only will it help any application, it will also allow you to decide whether this is really something you want to pursue in practice or whether you just like the idea in theory. Chapter 2 covers work experience in more depth, including how to find a placement.

Competition for places

In general, the number of UCAS applications continues to grow, with a total of 761,740 applications in 2022, an increase of 2% from 2021. UCAS states that in 2022, 92% of applicants received an offer. UCAS concludes this unusually high number of offers is a consequence of the removal of the cap on places and the decline in the size of the UK's school-leaver population. However, the competition for places at distinguished universities remains intense. Many candidates only gain places on an economics- or business-related course either through Clearing or by attending a lower-preference university. UCAS reports that, in 2022, 21,080 active applicants did not have a place on A level results day; however, 57% of them managed to subsequently secure a place through Clearing.

There is particularly strong competition for places on pure economics and pure management courses, with many more applicants than places available. Competitive courses at top-ranked universities can attract as many as 15 to 20 applications for every place. In 2021/22, the London School of Economics and Political Science (LSE) received 20 applications for each available place on its Economics and Economics History BSc programme. However, one in 15 applicants to the Economics BSc programme received an offer in 2021/22. This suggests it is worth checking acceptance rates for different programmes on university websites – selecting one variation of a course over another may give you a significant competitive advantage.

On average UK students are more successful in gaining UK university places than non-UK applicants. UCAS reports that in 2022, almost 80%

of UK applicants were offered places, compared to 47% of EU applicants and almost 50% of other international students. This could be due to better knowledge of the UCAS system and access to well-informed advisers. Also, most UK applicants sit A level exams while EU and other overseas applicants may rely upon their domestic exam results. Some admissions tutors may lack confidence that the qualifications of overseas students possess the academic rigour of A level courses.

The golfer Gary Player is said to have responded to accusations of being a 'lucky' golfer by saying 'the harder I work, the luckier I get'. Bear this in mind when considering your application to university. While there is a small element of luck involved in getting offers from universities, success is mainly down to planning (and, of course, working hard to achieve the best grades you can). You need to make sure you research your courses properly. Look at the websites of the universities you are considering and check if you are likely to meet the entry criteria. You can even contact them to ask for advice on how to strengthen your application through activities such as work experience. Because of the competition for places on highly ranked courses, it is particularly important to ensure that the personal statement section of your UCAS application is constructed carefully, and that your predicted grades are high enough for your first-choice university to consider you.

1 | Studying business, economics and related courses

For 2023/24 entry, UCAS lists 262 universities and colleges offering 4,451 business courses, 132 institutions offering 2,059 economics programmes, and 155 institutions offering 1,143 finance-related courses in the UK. So how do you decide which course is for you? This chapter looks at narrowing these courses down to the maximum of five that will end up on your UCAS application. It's a daunting prospect so we'll be looking at what questions you should be asking before you make that important final selection.

Different courses available

What's in a name?

You are considering a career in a business- or finance-related field, and you want to find a suitable university course that will help you achieve this. The university prospectuses that you sent off for have arrived, so you settle down in a comfortable chair to read through them and begin to make your choice of course. Two hours later, you are bewildered: should you choose business studies, business and management studies, management science or business management? What is the difference between banking and finance, and international banking? Would a potential employer favour economics over econometrics? Why do some universities offer mathematics with economics whereas others teach only mathematics and economics? Well, after reading this chapter you should have a clearer idea about the course you should consider.

Let us look at the courses listed on the website of that prestigious (but fictional!) institution, Barton University:

- accounting and finance
- banking and finance
- business and management studies
- business, mathematics and statistics

- business studies
- econometrics and mathematical economics
- economics
- financial economics
- management (three-year course)
- management (four-year sandwich course)
- management sciences
- mathematics and economics.

The first thing to be aware of is that there is considerable overlap between many of these courses. For example, as part of the business studies degree course, you would attend lectures on management – the same lectures that the management students attend. Additionally, in the second and third years of the course you will be offered options for the courses you wish to study, so you would be able to steer your degree towards the areas that interested you most. This brings us to the three important rules when it comes to choosing your courses:

- **Rule Number 1**. Read through the course content for all three or four years of the course. Do not choose a course just because of its title. You will find the content of a particular course varies from university to university, and that there is considerable choice available within a particular university's course. For example, the Economics course at Oxford is closely related to Politics and Philosophy as part of the renowned PPE course. However, the Cambridge Economics degree invariably highlights mathematical aspects, such as econometrics. This is important to know so you will choose a course which suits your interests and skills.

Similar-sounding courses often have different entrance requirements in terms of both preferred A level subjects and grade requirements. A degree in econometrics is likely to require a higher level of mathematical ability (possibly further mathematics to A level) than economics, and some universities will differentiate between their 'preferred' A level subjects (the more traditional A levels such as mathematics, history, physics or economics) and 'non-preferred' subjects (general studies, art and media studies are examples of subjects that some universities do not favour). Again, careful reading of the prospectus is important, because each university will have its own preferences or requirements.

The entrance requirements for degree courses will always specify what examination results are necessary. These are expressed either as grade requirements (for example, AAB) or Tariff points (for example, 136 – see Chapter 3). When you apply through UCAS (unless you are applying post-results; that is, during your gap year), your school or school UCAS adviser will put your predicted grades in your reference. You need to find out in advance what they are going to predict, because this will affect your choice of universities and courses. There is no point in applying for five university courses that require ABB if your A level predictions are CCC; you will be rejected by all of your choices and you will then need to try to find alternatives through the UCAS Extra scheme, or through Clearing (see Chapter 8). Similarly, if you are predicted to achieve AAA, you are probably aiming too low if all of the courses you are applying for require DDD at A level. As a rough guide, if you are predicted, say, ABB, you might want to choose three courses that require ABB, one that requires BBB and a course that demands BBC. This means that you have a good chance of getting a number of offers but it also gives you options if you do not quite meet the grade requirements when you get your results (see Chapter 8). If you want to apply for a course that requires grades higher than those you have been predicted, it might be worth contacting the admissions department at that university to ask for advice before completing your UCAS application. So, rules 2 and 3 are as follows.

- **Rule Number 2**. Research the entrance requirements for each course and for each university, and narrow down your options by finding the courses whose requirements most closely match your A level subjects and likely grades. International students must check the International English Language Testing System (IELTS) requirements. Universities may compromise on A Level grades, but they will not lower their IELTS demands.
- **Rule Number 3**. Find out what your grade predictions are and base your course choices on these.

We will now look at some of the Barton University courses in more detail. Bear in mind that courses with similar titles can differ significantly from university to university. These snapshots should be taken as an indication of what the courses involve but should not form the entirety of your research. Your choices should be based on a thorough investigation of each university's course details, using the prospectus or the website.

Accounting and finance

Accounting and finance courses look at the financial aspects of companies and businesses. You will study accounting techniques, how companies assess their financial performance and how they plan for the future. They also cover aspects of management, share dealing and the way companies are perceived by the public and by potential investors.

Courses you will take as part of the degree could include:

- elements of accounting and finance
- introduction to statistics
- managerial accounting
- principles of finance
- economic theories
- management science
- business mathematics
- commercial law.

Economics and econometrics

Economics is the study of income and expenditure, from small-scale situations (households or businesses) to global issues (how countries deal with income, spending, inflation and employment). It covers topics such as setting the price of goods, inflation, balance of payments and unemployment. Econometrics looks at how statistical methods are used to analyse and test economic theories. Students are also likely to study the economics of developing countries and inequality.

Courses you will take as part of the degree could include:

- microeconomics
- macroeconomics
- mathematical methods
- statistics
- econometrics
- development economics
- accounting and finance
- game theory
- international economics
- labour economics
- the history of economic thought.

Management

Management courses look at how organisations work effectively and cover a broad range of topics, such as the structure of an organisation, financial management and how people can be managed to get the best out of them. Management science is the study of how management methods are underpinned by analytical techniques and mathematical models.

Courses that you will take as part of your degree could include:

- economics
- psychology and behavioural science
- accounting and finance
- the process of management
- economics for management
- management science
- law.

Business studies

Business studies courses look at how businesses are run. A successful business model comprises a whole range of different aspects, from marketing, advertising, location and markets, through to financial issues and management. It is a practical rather than theoretical subject, focusing on problem solving and real-life situations.

Courses that you will take as part of your degree could include:

- accounting
- organisational behaviour
- economics
- management science
- a market or business project
- international business
- marketing.

As you can see, there is a great deal of crossover in the topics covered by these courses. A management degree will include some accounting, economics and business courses, and an economics degree will include aspects of accounting, management, finance and business. Business studies courses include modules on accounting, management and economics. Figure 1 will give you an indication of the links between these courses, and the differences between them.

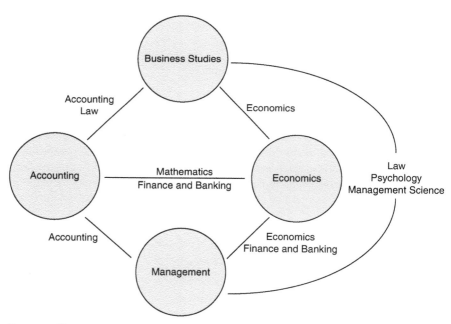

Figure 1 Degree courses showing common links between disciplines

Case study

'I will always remember learning about the basics of supply and demand in my first microeconomics lecture at university. Although A level Economics was not a prerequisite to studying the course at Durham, most of my peers had studied it at A level or IB, and I felt as though I was the only one who didn't know what was going on! I had to spend a little more time reading in those first few weeks than most other students, but I soon got up to speed. I'd recommend that others in that situation read some introductory books and get into the habit of reading a business-focused newspaper, such as the *Financial Times*, a couple of times a week during Upper Sixth – that would have really helped me. And don't worry, once you get through the first few weeks everyone is being exposed to new material and you are back on a level playing field.'

Rachel, Economics undergraduate student, Durham University

Single or joint honours?

When you start to look at specific courses you will find there are a range of different course types available. You may need to decide whether you want to opt for single honours, where you will specialise in one subject area, or joint honours, which will allow you to study more than one subject area and broaden your knowledge. Generally speaking, a single honours programme will prepare you better for a specific career and may enable you to work towards professional qualifications. Joint honours programmes may be a good option for those who are unsure about what career they would like to pursue after graduation.

Most business and management courses include the core subjects of finance, economics, law, marketing, management and human resources. Take a look at module options and decide whether you are happy to concentrate on these areas or whether you want to include some other element of study.

Joint honours options may come from a similar field or a completely different discipline. Pinpointing specific subjects that you would like to study in your degree can help narrow your choice of university. For example, you may want to consider adding a language to your course if you plan to work in an international environment in the future; or you may have a keen interest in a totally different area.

Some joint degrees do not require previous knowledge of the second subject. Others, especially those with a European language or a science-based discipline, often specify that candidates must have an A level or GCSE qualification, or equivalent, in a specific subject. In joint degrees, be wary of courses that have similar titles, such as 'Business with German' and 'Business and German'. In the former, business is the major subject and German is the minor, but in the second, which is more likely to involve a year abroad, you will probably spend equal time on each subject. Economics and mathematical subjects go well together because economics is a theoretical subject, underpinned by mathematics and statistical methods. You will find a wide range of courses that combine economics with mathematics and/or statistics. For strong mathematicians, some of these courses may be easier to get offers for than the single honours economics courses. However, do not think that this is an easy way to get to study economics at a top university. These degrees will involve the study of mathematical topics to a high level, and so you need to be interested in mathematical subjects (and good at them) to get on to this type of course.

Case study

'When I tell people that I graduated with a joint honours degree (Business Studies with Media and Culture), I'm often greeted with some baffled responses because they are two completely different subjects, people don't see the connection between the two and, consequently, think that the lack of clear connection is a bad thing. But, after explaining how many different opportunities doing two different courses gave me, and that I now have the option to move into a broad and varied range of jobs, people are quick to change their opinion. Graduating with joint honours simply means that I have one degree in two subjects. Employers don't see a joint honours degree in a negative way or as only 50% of one subject. In fact, having a degree in two subjects can increase your chances of finding work when you graduate. It can be beneficial for going into teaching because you can show potential employers that you have expertise in two subjects, and so can apply for jobs in two different areas.

'When choosing a single honours course, the classes that you can choose are more fixed. Whereas a joint honours degree allows you to pick and choose the modules that you want to do, giving you more flexibility. Therefore, if there are certain classes you won't enjoy, or won't be very good at, you can miss those out (providing it's not a mandatory module) and pick one that suits you, as long as your timetable allows you to do so.'

Alex, University of Worcester

Professional accreditation

Are you thinking about going into accountancy, banking or insurance? Most commerce-related degrees contain modules that will give you exemptions from some of the examinations that aspiring professionals are obliged to sit for organisations such as the Chartered Institute of

Marketing, the Chartered Institute of Personnel and Development and the various accountancy bodies. If you are concerned about which exemption subjects you can include in your degree, call the universities and ask which of the professional bodies recognise their courses.

Alternatively, you can get in touch with individual professional bodies directly and they will tell you which university courses are officially accredited. Although taking exemptions as part of a degree course can be convenient, it is not disastrous for your career if you don't – but your professional qualifications may take an extra six months to complete.

Sandwich degrees

A sandwich degree is typically four years long, with the third year spent on placement. The kind of placement will depend on your course and your area of interest. A foreign-language student may study at an overseas university; a business student may go to work for a company for the year. You would return to complete your degree in the fourth year and will gain credit for your time on placement. The real advantage of a sandwich year is that when you graduate you will already have some commercial experience, which will help you stand out when applying for jobs or graduate schemes. It is well worth researching what kind of support your chosen universities offer to their sandwich students. Find out what industrial links they have: do they have a placement office to help you secure relevant experience and what have previous graduates from the same course gone on to achieve?

Degree apprenticeships

A degree apprenticeship is a relatively new qualification which combines academia with real-world, industrial experience. Students study part time at university while also working for an employer, and can achieve a full bachelor's (or master's) degree upon completion of the apprenticeship. For example, the supermarket Morrisons has partnered with the universities of Bradford and Strathclyde to offer a three-year degree apprenticeship programme in retail, logistics, corporate and manufacturing. They cover the tuition costs for various part-time degrees, such as BSc (Hons) Management and Business at the University of Bradford.

This type of qualification works particularly well for those students who prefer to integrate practice and theory, and wish to apply their technical knowledge in a real-world context day in, day out. The employer also pays the apprentice a salary and covers the cost of the apprentice's part-time university studies, which is a hugely attractive proposition for many young people. However, it is important to consider the challenges of balancing multiple commitments. The experience will not be like that of regular university students, who effectively manage their own time and studies; apprentices will take on real roles within real businesses, and be responsible for a number of deliverables.

Many employers have embraced degree apprenticeships – it allows them to grow their own talent and embed good candidates into the company from an early stage. An apprentice's education is tailored to the business that they will join. UCAS reports an increased demand for apprenticeship opportunities in 2022 – compared to a previous year, there were almost 22% more clicks in UCAS Career Finder.

You can learn more about degree apprenticeships at www.ucas.com/apprenticeships/degree-apprenticeships. Further, UCAS, in partnership with the consumer organisation Which? and the National Apprenticeship Service, has published a guide to higher and degree apprenticeships, which is available at www.ucas.com/file/301156/download?token=lkr35v3v.

Overseas study

The opportunity to study abroad could also be a factor that affects your degree selection. It is possible to study business and management in dozens of countries across the globe as part of a degree based at a British university. Not all of these courses send you off for a full year, though: there are schemes that last for only one term or a semester. You do not need to be a linguist either, because it is always possible to study overseas in an English-speaking location such as North America, South Africa, Australia or Malaysia. The popularity of overseas study has encouraged some universities to develop special exchange relationships with universities further afield.

Methods of assessment and study

Degrees are usually assessed through a combination of examinations (normally spread over two or three years) and coursework, although individual units may be assessed purely by coursework or dissertation. Methods of studying, such as lectures, seminars, tutorials, practicals, workshops and self-study, tend not to vary much between universities (except for Oxford and Cambridge, where they centre on the one-to-one tutorial system). Some institutions, however, do offer part-time courses and even distance learning for a few of their degrees.

2 | Getting work experience

It is no secret that university admissions tutors like work experience. Being able to demonstrate your commitment to and knowledge of your chosen area could mean the difference between being offered a place on a course or not. It was challenging to secure work experience during the Covid-19 pandemic, with limited opportunities via virtual delivery methods. As stated in High Fliers Research, there has been a surge in work experience opportunities in 2022 as a result of most Covid-19 restrictions being lifted. However, some placements and taster programmes will continue to be offered virtually. This chapter will look at using work experience to make your UCAS application stand out and the importance of getting internships and work placements while at university.

Work experience

Getting some relevant work experience has become more valuable in recent years, and is considered essential by some university admissions tutors. In a climate where getting into business, economics or management is so fiercely competitive, it is not enough just to be a brilliant academic. One of the things that an admissions tutor will look for is how serious you are about your chosen course. Many students decide to apply for a business- or finance-related course at university because they think it will be an easy route to becoming rich rather than because they are actually interested in the course content and the skills that they will acquire from their studies. Work experience or work shadowing is an ideal way to demonstrate your commitment and show that you have done some research. Several organisations now also offer virtual experience, which can be as valuable as traditional face-to-face volunteering, work or internship opportunities. If you can recount on your personal statement and in interviews what you saw or did on your work placement, and how those experiences related to your A level studies, proposed university course or future career, you will be a much more attractive proposition to the university selectors.

If you have decided to take a gap year, it is a good idea to spend part of it gaining experience relevant to your degree. This will be valuable during your course and will appeal to employers once you have graduated.

In addition, the more (ideally relevant) experience you have, the better your chance of succeeding in your initial job applications. Many employers will rate work experience as being almost as important as academic qualifications.

What will you gain from work experience?

- It adds weight to your personal statement.
- It gives you a true insight into the business or financial world and whether or not it is what you want to do. Some real experience will be particularly useful if you are trying to weigh up which area of business you'd like to go into. For example, are you more analytical or creative? Would you be more suited to a career in finance or marketing?
- It helps you to make a better transition from education into the world of full-time work.
- It gives you the opportunity to build up those all-important contacts.
- It gives you a more impressive curriculum vitae (CV) – and will help you to gain excellent references (with luck!), both of which are important for any future career.

However, it is not that easy getting relevant work experience. Most admissions tutors and employers recognise this and do not stipulate that it is essential, although it is preferred. If you cannot get experience in a large business, any work experience that demonstrates your use of the skills employers are interested in will be valuable. Working as waiting staff, for example, will demonstrate commercial awareness, experience in customer service and an appreciation of how a business is structured. Communication skills, determination, commercial awareness and IT skills can all be developed in many other sectors of business and commerce.

'Your extra-curricular activities such as work experience ... are important, particularly when they can provide evidence of useful skills such as problem solving, working under pressure and time management ....'

London School of Economics

'All the candidates' interests outside their academic studies assist selection by providing valuable background information.'

Imperial College, London

'We need to see evidence that your interest is genuine: If a degree is related to a particular line of work, that you have work experience ... or can demonstrate you understand what the profession involves.'

University of Birmingham

Looking for work experience

There are a number of volunteering bodies which will enable you to connect with potential placements. Do-it (www.do-it.life/volunteer) has a search function so you can browse opportunities by area. There are a number of volunteering organisations aimed specifically at young people. The National Citizen Service (www.ncsyes.co.uk) is aimed at 16–17-year-olds interested in supporting their local community. The National Council for Voluntary Youth Service (www.ncvys.org.uk), Volunteering Matters (www.volunteeringmatters.org.uk), RateMy Placement (www.ratemyplacement.co.uk), Student Volunteers UK (www.studenthubs.org) and Student Ladder (www.studentladder.co.uk) are also excellent places for young people to look. Young Professionals (www.young-professionals.uk) offers great events, talks and work experience opportunities with major UK and global employers. Also, Spring Pod (www.springpod.com) has a wealth of work experience, both face to face and online, allowing you to gain experience with top employers and universities for free. First Careers (www.firstcareers. co.uk/work-experience-opportunities) lists work experience opportunities at some of the largest and most successful UK companies, e.g. Asda, Barclays and Deloitte. In most instances, First Careers will redirect you to the company website, through which you can make your application.

You may also want to approach companies and organisations directly. It is wise to ask friends and family for any advice or contacts they might have which could be useful. Otherwise, look at your local jobs website to get an idea of what kind of businesses there are in your area and contact the human resources department to ask if they might consider providing you with work experience.

If your school offers Young Enterprise (www.young-enterprise.org.uk), it is worth getting involved in the scheme if you are considering studying for a business- or economics-related degree. The organisation may also be able to offer advice on how to progress in the world of business and finance, having provided nearly 400,000 students of all ages with practical experience of work and business. If you are struggling to find valuable and relevant work experience, Young Enterprise offers a viable alternative which is likely to impress admissions tutors.

Since the Covid-19 pandemic, many companies offer virtual (and usually free) work experience. Compared with face-to-face work opportunities, these can offer a lot of flexibility. Their virtual nature allows students to work across the country and even the globe. Websites such as www.prospects.ac.uk provide a lot of useful information on virtual work experience, including the names of current employers offering such work experience and internship opportunities.

Where to look and what to expect

There is no single guaranteed way of getting work experience, so try as many ways as you can think of, and be creative in the process. Here are a few suggestions.

- Ask your teachers at school/college if they have any contacts in the business world.
- Use your careers library and speak to your careers officer.
- Talk to your family and friends and ask them whether they can suggest anyone worth contacting.
- Make sure everyone you know is aware you are looking for work experience.
- Send your CV and a covering letter to a variety of local businesses.
- Keep up to date by reading the business pages of the quality press.
- Watch and listen to the business programmes on television and radio.
- Do your own online research – new information appears regularly, and more companies now offer online opportunities worldwide.

If you have a contact in a local organisation, try asking to go in for one or two weeks' work experience during the holidays, or even ask for one day's work-shadowing to get an insight into what the business environment is like. Whichever route you take, it will almost certainly be on a voluntary basis unless you have specific skills to offer, such as good office and keyboard skills. If that is the case, you could try to get some paid work during the summer or register with an employment agency.

How to put together a CV to apply for work experience

It is never too early to start to put together a CV. This is a summary of what you have done in your life to date. If you are a mature would-be student with a lot of jobs behind you, there is sometimes a case for going on to a second page, but for most young people a brief CV will be appropriate. The main headings to cover are described below.

Name and contact details

These are the basic details to head your CV. Make sure they're right!

Education and qualifications

Start with your present course of study and work back to the beginning of secondary school. No primary schools please! List the qualifications with grades you already have and the ones you intend to sit.

Work experience

Start with the most recent. Don't worry if you have had only a Saturday job at the local shop or a paper round. Put it all down. Employers would rather see that you have done something, and every job will teach you some skills, such as reliability or retail skills.

Skills

List everything you do that could have a commercial application, such as computer skills, software packages used, typing, languages, driving licence and so on.

Interests and positions of responsibility

What do you like to do in your spare time? If you hold or have held any positions of responsibility, such as captain of a sports team, been a committee member or head boy or girl at school, put it all down. Do you play an instrument or have a creative hobby? Do you belong to a society or club? All these say something about the person you are.

Referees

You should usually mention two referees: an academic one, such as a teacher or head of your school, plus someone who knows you well personally but is not a relative, such as someone you have worked for.

Always highlight your good points on a CV and do not leave gaps. Always account for your time. If something such as illness prevented you from reaching your potential in your exams, point this out in your covering letter. To succeed in business you need to have excellent attention to detail, so make sure your spelling and grammar are perfect! Lay out your CV clearly and logically and include any exams you are studying for as well as those you have already taken. The box below offers an example.

Gabriella Jones
Tel 07123 456789; **Email** g.jones@email.com
Address 12 Miles Road, Cambridge CB1 2AB

Education
Mander Portman Woodward (2021–2023)
3 A levels: Maths, Further Maths, Economics – grades pending
7 GCSEs: English Lit (8), English Lang (8), Physics (8), Biology (6), Mathematics (6), History (6), Art (8)

Work experience
John Lewis, Cambridge (August 2022)
Two weeks in the Womenswear department.

Royal High Academy, Cambridge (August 2022)
Three weeks as temporary receptionist in a school, answering calls and dealing with enquiries.

Duck Pond Café, Cambridge (July 2021–present)
Part-time barista and waiting staff.

Skills and Achievements
Maths Senior Challenge – gold award (2022)
Duke of Edinburgh Bronze Award
Languages: Spanish (CEFR level B2)
European Computer Driving Licence (ARU, 2019)
Shortlisted for Fitzwilliam College Cambridge Land Economy Essay Competition

Positions of responsibility
School prefect in Sixth Form.
Treasurer for Young Enterprise company.

Interests
Mixed football, yoga, reading, and cooking.

References
Available on request.

The covering letter/formal email

Most applications are currently online, and usually include a suitability section where candidates can talk about their suitability for the job. Some candidates are asked to upload their CV and write a covering letter, which they send via email. Formal emails have also become a crucial part of modern-day communication.

The formal letter/email is important because it is usually the first thing a potential employer reads. Here are some tips on its structure and format.

- It is written in formal language with a specific format for business purpose. It is formal in style and register, and uses a tone that is clear and polite.
- Try to find out the name of the person to whom you should send your formal letter and CV. It makes a great difference to the reader if you can personalise your application – but do not be overly familiar. Use their title (Mr, Ms, Dr, etc.) and last name, not 'Dear Bob'. (Get a book on business letter writing if you need help with the conventions. For example, if you start the letter 'Dear Mr Brown' remember you should finish it 'Yours sincerely'. If you do not know the recipient's name and send it, for example, to the personnel manager, begin with 'Dear Sir or Madam' and finish with 'Yours faithfully'.)
- The first paragraph should tell the reader why you are contacting them (e.g. 'I am writing to enquire whether you have any openings for work experience').
- The second paragraph should attempt to engage them by highlighting your interest in business, along with some specific skills you can

offer, such as knowledge of word processing or having a good telephone manner.

- Say in the letter whether you know anything about the company and how you found out about it (e.g. if friends or family work there) or whether you've read anything recently that was of interest or was relevant to your career prospects.
- Covering letters are usually typed into an email or sent as a separate attachment.

Whether you are applying for a position through an advertisement or just sending a speculative email or letter to a local company, you should do plenty of research on the employer. Having some information will help you tailor your CV for that particular company, and it will certainly be impressive if at an interview you show some knowledge of how the company works.

If you have an application form to fill in, follow the instructions carefully and make sure that you take your time; a sloppy application will not be helpful, even if the content makes you a strong candidate. You probably won't be asked to submit your CV as well, so always include evidence about your skills and interests in the statements on your application form.

It is imperative that you keep copies of all correspondence, CVs and application forms you send off, not just so you can remember to whom you have applied but so that you have something to work from at an interview. You are bound to be asked to elaborate on things you have written about yourself, so do not say you have a skill or an interest if you cannot back it up.

Work experience interviews

Most of the tips from Chapter 6 are equally useful if you are going for a work experience interview. However, here are some additional pointers.

- Think through why you want the job, and in particular why you want to work for that organisation.
- Research the employer thoroughly before the interview. Look at their brochure and website.
- Plan in advance what you think your key selling points are for the employer and make sure you find an opportunity in the interview to get these across.
- Think up a few relevant questions to ask your interviewer at the end. You can demonstrate your preparation here by asking them about something you have read about the company recently, if appropriate.
- Dress smartly, but not too formal.

- Sit up straight, look at the person speaking, and answer in clear and simple language. Humour is best avoided.
- Offer a nice, firm, confident handshake at the beginning and end of the interview.
- Be confident without lapsing into arrogance.

Making the most of your work experience

You've gone through all of the above steps to secure yourself a work experience placement, but simply having spent some time in a business is not enough. You need to make sure you can demonstrate exactly what you have got from the experience. Here are some tips for making your experience really count.

1. **Keep a diary**. It will help you to remember what you did and, more importantly, what you learned from your experiences. You'll be able to draw on it when writing your personal statement and going to any interviews. Saying you have picked up new skills is almost useless without evidence, so writing things down will mean you can back up your claims later.

2. **Impress**. It isn't enough to just be there: make sure you are on time, presentable and enthusiastic. The employer will want to know that you value the experience, so show them that you are taking it seriously.

3. **Be seen to be enthusiastic and professional**. Those around you are likely to be busy, so you may need to get yourself noticed (in a good way!). If you have finished something, make sure you ask for something else to do, and ask questions to show that you are interested in what you are doing.

4. **Behave appropriately**. Being friendly is essential, but make sure you keep it professional. You are not there to make friends but to get valuable experience, so don't get drawn into office politics and remember you could need to call on any of your colleagues for help or as a reference at some point in the future.

5. **Be organised**. If you do all your work excellently but leave a trail of scrap paper everywhere you will be remembered for the wrong reasons.

6. **Network.** We're not talking about adding your new boss on Facebook (see number 4 – behave appropriately!); this is about making a good impression so that you can come back to people if it might be useful later on. You'll be surprised how often you'll need to call on the help of others for references or advice, and those who get ahead seem to have networking down to a fine art. Before you leave, ask key staff if you could take their email addresses and if they would mind you contacting them if you need advice. You may also consider creating a LinkedIn profile (www.linkedin.com) and adding staff you've come into contact with as LinkedIn contacts.

If you think it would be useful to get more experience at the company or an internship (see below), ask your employer if there might be any opportunities coming up.

Internships

Internships and work placements play a crucial role in the recruitment of new graduates. The gruelling recruitment process for graduates in their penultimate year of university is often very similar to the recruitment process for interns in their first or second years at university. Recruiters will therefore often offer their interns places on the coveted graduate scheme, and hold it for them while they complete their degree. Gaining a place on a competitive internship, and possibly a subsequent offer to join that firm as a graduate, will take huge amounts of pressure off you in your final year at university, when many undergraduates are juggling their dissertation, final exams and job applications.

High Fliers Research conducted a study entitled *The Graduate Market in 2022*, in which it was reported that, due to the Covid-19 pandemic, employers cut their graduate intake by more than 12% in 2020. Encouragingly, employers in many industries, including the business sector, are set to expand their recruitment in 2022. Compared to the pre-pandemic peak back in 2019, the number of graduate vacancies available now is 11% higher.

The latest recruitment targets for the country's leading employers show that the number of graduate jobs on offer in 2022 is expected to increase by 15.7% from 2021, the largest annual rise in graduate recruitment for more than 15 years. It is expected that accounting and professional services firms will be the biggest recruiters of new graduates in 2022.

Interestingly, despite the fact that almost 60% of the UK's top employers are planning to recruit more graduates, the same study found that almost half the employers taking part in the research reported there has been a drop in graduate work experience applications for their placements, internships and taster courses in 2022. This shows just how important work experience is for graduate recruiters. With this in mind, it is certainly worth checking what sort of career support is available at the universities you are considering. Will they help you find a placement? What are the graduate employment figures like? Is there an opportunity to do a year in industry? Employers will attend a large number of university campuses to promote their intern and graduate opportunities. The High Fliers Report 2022 states that the top five universities currently targeted by many leading graduate employers are Manchester, Nottingham, Bristol, Birmingham and Leeds. Interestingly, three universities on this list – Manchester, Birmingham and Nottingham

– are only ranked 23rd, 25th and 28th respectively in *The Times and The Sunday Times Good University Guide 2022*.

Internships come in all shapes and sizes. Some are over the summer holidays – often referred to as 'Summer Analyst' programmes – while some are part time alongside your studies, particularly after the second year of a course. Many companies are making internships available to first-year undergraduates (in the banking world, these week-long paid internships are referred to as Spring Week).

The majority of the UK's top graduate employers have made good use of social media since the pandemic, with 20% of recruiters referring to social media promotions as 'very successful'. Almost 90% have used commercial graduate recruitment websites (such as TARGETJobs, Bright Network and Gradcracker) and graduate directories (such as *The Times Top 100 Graduate Employers* and *Prospects Student Career Guide*).

It's never too early to start making links, as finding a work placement can often be half the battle. Opening up useful contacts by doing volunteering and work experience before university could prove very beneficial. Check with your local volunteering office or look at the following websites for information and ideas:

- Volunteering Matters: www.volunteeringmatters.org.uk
- Do-it: www.do-it.life/volunteer
- Voluntary Service Overseas (VSO): www.vsointernational.org.

Case study

'During the first term of my first year at Bristol University, studying Economics, I applied to Bank of America Merrill Lynch's (BAML's) Spring Week programme and was given a place. During the Easter holidays, I spent a week at BAML's headquarters in London, rotating around different teams in the investment bank and was tasked with various group activities and presentations. At the end of the week, I was offered a place on the BAML summer internship for the following year. Following a successful summer internship, I was offered a place on their Graduate Scheme, to begin the same year I graduated. It was amazing to have this job lined up for me during my final year; it allowed me to really focus on writing my dissertation and studying for my final exams.'

Tom, Economics graduate, University of Bristol

---

3 | Choosing your course

You should remember that a degree in business, economics or management is not always a prerequisite for a specific role, nor is it a guarantee of a high-flying job. However, these courses provide an excellent foundation and may give you a head start in the world of business or finance over other graduates. Some courses are biased towards particular areas – such as econometrics, marketing or personnel. If you already have an interest in a particular area, look for courses where this will be drawn out and developed.

Many potential employers are more interested in the class of a degree than its subject. If you do want to get into business but do not want to take business studies, it should not matter that much – as long as you do well in what you do and end up with a minimum of a 2.i degree. But if you are set on studying business, economics or management at degree level, read on – because there are a huge number of courses available and you will need to do some serious planning.

What to consider

You are allowed five choices on the UCAS form. The basic factors to consider when choosing your degree course are:

- the kind of business, economics, management, finance or related course you are looking for
- where you want to study
- your academic ability.

Going to university is an investment for your future and you need to squeeze the most out of your time there, so it pays to think hard about these points. They are all essential in helping you through the lengthy task of selecting what to study and where. Given the huge number of institutions offering business, economics and management courses, it is advisable to start by narrowing your options down to between 10 and 20. To reduce the vast array of business and economics courses to a reasonable number you should establish your predicted grades and choose universities that are likely to make you an offer.

- Contact your chosen universities or colleges and ask for their prospectuses (both official and alternative) and departmental brochures (if they exist) for more details. Remember that the universities' publications are promotional and may be selective about the information they provide.
- Visit the websites of the universities you are considering. These often contain more up-to-date information than the prospectuses.
- Attend university open days if you can, and talk to former or current students. Try to imagine whether you would be happy living for three or four years in that environment. You should consider issues such as whether you'd prefer to be on a campus or in a city, and whether there are facilities for you to pursue your other interests and hobbies.
- Talk to any people in business that you know and ask for their views on the reputations of different universities and courses.
- Find out what academic criteria your shortlisted universities are looking for and be realistic about the grades you are expecting. Your teachers at school or college will be able to advise you on this.
- Make sure the course allows you to select any particular options you are interested in by thoroughly checking out what is available. The list can sometimes be mind-boggling! You will not always know what each option actually covers from its title, so read the department's own prospectus carefully and address any unanswered questions by contacting the admissions tutors directly.
- Think about whether or not you would like a course that includes an industrial placement. This can give you extremely valuable experience and is a great opportunity to make useful contacts for the future (see Chapter 2). Employers also like graduates who have had a practical placement. If you do choose such a course, it is well worth your while checking whose responsibility it is to find you a placement: does the university have a placement officer who will help you with this process, or is it entirely up to you to find something?
- Do you want to spend some time abroad? If you are doing a course that has some foreign-language content, it might be possible to do a work placement in that country. This could be particularly valuable, as you would not only gain practical work experience but also improve your language skills, which could give you the edge when you come to look for a job after graduation.
- Try to find out about the reputation of the academic staff. If you are going to be taking a business and management degree, you might prefer to be taught by academics who have some experience of business themselves. Use the internet to find out what experience they have and what they've published.

League tables

When you are trying to select your five university choices, you may find university league tables helpful, as they will give you an indication of how a university or a course is regarded. A word of warning though – there are no official rankings of universities. The tables are normally compiled by the national newspapers and are based on a whole range of criteria. No two league tables will rank each university in the same way, nor will they produce the same results. However, they are a useful source of information, and might be one of the resources you use when making your choices. Tables on the *Guardian* website (www.theguardian.com/education) can be reordered by clicking on the category that you think is most important. For example, you could look at the economics ranking ordered by the entrance grades of students being accepted on to the course (a good indication of the quality of the students). You could also look at the ranking by job prospects, based on the destinations of graduates six months after graduating.

Other league tables that you might find useful include those produced by the *Times* (www.thetimes.co.uk or www.timeshighereducation.co.uk) and the Complete University Guide (www.thecompleteuniversityguide.co.uk).

Once you have thoroughly researched the options available, you should have a shortlist of universities that fulfil your criteria – the course that suits your needs, the right locations, and the ability to pursue your interests. From that, you can choose the top five places to put in your UCAS application. You need to consider the entry requirements and your chances of securing the exam grades needed; you can find this information on the university website under the entry criteria. It is sensible to plan for one or two top choices (requiring grades you know you achieve on a good day when the odds are in your favour), one or two 'doable' choices, and one or two safe options (with lower entry criteria compared to your other options).

Other rankings and statistics

The National Student Survey is a big questionnaire completed by graduates all over the UK. It's really useful as it gives you a student perspective on what life is like at any given university. Results are published only for departments with over 50% survey completion, and they can be viewed online at www.officeforstudents.org.uk.

The 'Higher Education Policy Institute Student Academic Experience Survey 2022' states that only 35% of students felt they received good or very good value for money; the survey also found that the quality of teaching was the most important indicator.

The TEF (The Teaching Excellence and Student Outcomes Framework) provides an independent assessment of the quality of courses by academic experts and students. Gold, Silver and Bronze ratings incentivise providers to achieve excellence in quality of teaching, the learning environment, and the educational and professional outcomes achieved by students.

Universities check up on their students six months after they have graduated to see what proportion have found work, are continuing their studies, are having a gap year or are unemployed. Graduate employability figures can also be viewed at www.officeforstudents.org.uk. Make sure you look at the full data, as the information in the league tables is just an overview to give an indication of graduate prospects. The Office for Students website also allows you to look at student breakdown (including the male to female ratio), degree classifications and how many UCAS points successful applicants came to the course with.

For those who want to dig a little deeper, you can always check out the latest QAA (Quality Assurance Agency) report on a particular university. This is the body that inspects universities and publishes findings on how institutions manage the quality of their qualifications. See www.qaa. ac.uk for more information.

The next section outlines an assortment of factors that might have some bearing on where you would like to study. See which are relevant to you and try to put them in order of importance.

Academic and career-related factors

Your academic ability

For the majority of students, their A level scores will be the deciding criterion for selection. It is important to be realistic about the grades you are heading for: do not be too pessimistic, but do not delude yourself about the risk you would be taking if you overstate your academic performance. Talk to your teachers for an accurate picture of your predicted results. Some places specify particular grades but will still take you on if you get the same Tariff point score. So, for example, if you are supposed to get BBB (which amounts to 3 × 40 = 120 points), then any combination that produces 120 points (i.e. ABC or AAD) may be acceptable. However, you should not assume this and should always check with the university of your choice.

Full details of the UCAS Tariff point system can be found on the UCAS website. In basic terms, the Tariff system attempts to compare different qualifications by attributing a point score. For example, an A grade at A level is worth 48 points and a B grade is worth 40 points. A grade 7 at International Baccalaureate Higher Level and a Scottish Advanced Higher grade A are both worth 56 points.

When you receive your offers, your universities will often specify what they would like you to achieve in order to confirm your place. A given university might ask for 120 points, and the offer might also specify that this applies to three A level subjects (if this is what you are studying). To satisfy the offer, the student would need to achieve at least ABC, AAD or BBB or some specified combination to attain this total.

If you receive a 'points' offer from a university, you should ensure that you are clear whether it includes just the A level grades, the A level and AS grades (if appropriate), or whether other qualifications that attract UCAS Tariff points (such as Key Skills or certain music examinations) can be included as well. However, most distinguished universities will only be interested in your A level grades or equivalent qualifications.

Educational facilities

Is there a well-stocked and up-to-date business library nearby, or will you have to fight other business and management students for the materials? Check for computer access if you do not have your own or in case there is no internet access in your student accommodation. If you are taking a joint degree involving sciences or languages, make sure there are facilities for your other subjects, such as science or language laboratories. The facilities available will depend on the budget of an institution, and plentiful resources tend to attract better tutors.

Quality of teaching

This is difficult to establish without the benefit of an open day, but the Higher Education Funding Council for England, the Higher Education Funding Council for Wales, the Scottish Funding Council and the Department for Education and Learning of Northern Ireland have done the groundwork for you and have assessed the level of teaching across the UK already. Their findings are publicly available – see www.office forstudents.org.uk, www.hefcw.ac.uk and www.sfc.ac.uk.

Teaching quality can suffer if seminar or tutorial groups are too large, so try to compare group sizes for the same courses at different institutions.

Type of institution

There are essentially three types of degree-awarding institutions: the 'old' universities, the 'new' universities and the colleges of higher education. There are also some private universities.

The 'old' universities

Traditionally the more academic universities, usually with higher admission requirements, the old universities are well established, with good libraries and research facilities. They have a reputation for being resistant to change, but most have introduced modern elements into their degrees such as modular courses, and an academic year split into two semesters.

The 'new' universities

Before 1992, these institutions were polytechnics, institutes or colleges. They form a separate group because they tend to still hold true to the original polytechnic mission of vocational courses and strong ties with industry, typically through placements and work experience. Because of this there are a number of excellent business and management degree courses at new universities that are very well regarded and entry is highly competitive. Some are still looked down on by certain employers because of their generally lower academic entry requirements, but the new universities have a good name for flexible admissions and learning, modern approaches to their degrees and good pastoral care.

Colleges of higher education

These are sometimes specialist institutions that provide excellent facilities in their chosen fields, despite their size. They are sometimes affiliated to universities. This form of franchising means that the college buys the right to teach the degree, which the university will award provided that the course meets the standards set by the university.

Private universities

There are a number of private universities in the UK that either have their own degree-awarding powers or whose degrees are awarded by an overseas university. These include the University of Buckingham, BPP University College, Regent's University, the University of Law, Arden University and New York University in London, among others. Private universities are not funded by the government and are free to set their own tuition fees, so you will need to check this with each institution. These institutions may also have their own applications procedure; contact them directly for further information. The rise in tuition fees in non-private universities has made private institutions a more attractive proposition in recent years.

Attractiveness to employers

Few employers will openly admit to giving preference to graduates from particular universities. Most are looking for high-quality degrees, often a 2.i or above, as an indication of strong academic ability. But, since students with higher A level grades have tended to go to the old universities, it is unsurprising that a large proportion of successful business people come from traditional university backgrounds.

A bit of research you can do yourself is to find out how past students have fared in the employment market. Ask to look at the university's annual final destinations survey, which should be available from its careers service or the department itself.

Distance learning

The vast majority of students choose to study full time and complete their degrees in the shortest possible period. However, if you are a mature student or it would be more convenient to your circumstances, you might wish to explore the option of distance learning. According to the Distance Learning Portal (www.distancelearningportal.com), there are over 2,000 business- and management-related distance learning degrees to choose from in the UK, and the growth of the internet will only increase this number in the years ahead.

The University of East London supports a BA in Business; there 'students can take a shorter or longer time to complete the degree according to their needs and inclination'. However, students are normally expected to study one or two modules at any one time and take a minimum of three years to complete all 18 units. For example, the University of Essex offers an online BA degree in Business and Management, which has entry requirements of either two A levels or equivalent, or GCSE Maths and English at grade 4 combined with three years' relevant work experience. The course has an indicative study duration of four years, but the actual duration may vary depending on a student's personal circumstances and study options.

The University of London, with academic direction from LSE (London School of Economics and Political Science), is offering part-time, online BSc degrees with four start dates per year in nine different courses, such as International Business, Business and Economics, Economics, Data Science and Business Analytics. Successful candidates need to meet the general and academic entry requirements including A level Mathematics and a certain English language level.

The Open University (OU), the University of Derby, the University of Sunderland, Birmingham City University and the University of Bradford also offer distance learning courses while the University of Liverpool, along with the University of Leicester, offers master's courses. The University of Essex is offering a BSc degree in Law with Business, which gives insight into law as well as business and management topics.

Non-academic considerations

Location

While some students have a clear picture of where they want to study, others are fairly geographically mobile, preferring instead to concentrate on choosing the right degree course and then seeing where they end up. But university life is not going to be solely about academic study. It is truly a growing experience – educationally, socially, culturally – and besides, three or four years can really drag if you are not happy outside the lecture theatre. The course search tool on the UCAS website is a good starting point because you can begin your search by specifying the regions in the UK where you would like to study.

Finances

The cost of living is not the same across the UK, so you should consider whether you will be able to reach deeper into your pockets for rent or other fundamentals and entertainment if you are living in a big city or in the south of England.

Friends and family

Do you want to get away from them or stay as close as possible? While there can be advantages, financial at least, to living at home, you might prefer the challenge of looking after yourself and the opportunity to be completely independent. You could have deeply personal reasons for applying to a particular university, but it is not a good idea to go to an institution just because your best friend is studying there.

Accommodation

Do you want to live in halls of residence with other students, or in private housing that you might need to organise yourself and could be a considerable distance from your place of study? Most institutions have an accommodation officer who will help you find a suitable place to live; and many universities will guarantee a room in halls of residence to first-year students anyway. But you will probably have to fend for yourself at some stage, so check on the availability of student housing, the cost and the distance from the university. If your university is nearby, is there any point moving away from home?

Leisure and entertainment

Are you going to be spending much time in, for example, the sports centre, the theatre or student bars? How about university societies – is there one that allows you to indulge your existing hobbies or caters for those you have always dreamt of trying?

Site and size

Many universities overcome the problems of urban versus rural and small versus large by locating their campuses on the edge of a major town (e.g. the University of Nottingham and the University of Kent) and centralising certain facilities and services to ensure safety, convenience and some sense of community, even on the largest and most widespread campus. However, some students prefer to feel they are part of the local town or city community, rather than being isolated on an out-of-town site. The bigger single-campus universities might cover a larger area than some of the smaller multi-site institutions. And do not be put off by the expression 'multi-site' – individual sites are likely to be self-contained, so students do not have to travel to other sites too often.

Case study

'I chose to study economics at university as I was interested in international politics and economics. I wasn't sure what I wanted to do after I graduated and thought an economics degree would leave my options pretty open. I was surprised by the variety of subjects I covered, and although I liked this about my course not all of my classmates agreed. I would recommend looking carefully at the degree structure and module choice before deciding on your university as content can vary quite widely between institutions. I had taken a gap year before university and wanted to graduate as soon as possible so didn't consider a year in industry. Looking back, I wish I hadn't been in such a rush, as my friends on the sandwich course benefited from lots of relevant industrial experience. I feel I could have progressed quicker in my first couple of years after graduation had I completed a placement.'

Sarah, BSc Economics graduate, University College London

4 | The UCAS application

The following advice should help you complete your UCAS application. More specific advice on filling in your application is given in *How to Complete Your UCAS Application* (Trotman Education).

While all information is correct at the time of writing, in January 2023 UCAS released its report *Future of Undergraduate Admission* outlining a number of potential reforms to the application process, most notably to the format of the reference and the replacement of the 4,000-character personal statement with a set of questions. Further details are yet to be announced, but the personal statement changes will be introduced no earlier than the 2024 application cycle (for 2025 entry).

The application

The UCAS application is completed on the UCAS website. UCAS Hub (previously known as UCAS Track) is UCAS's online applications system, which you use to register and apply to your university choices. You can sign in to your Hub to check your application's progress at any time, including to view any interview invitations and offers you receive. There are 11 sections to complete on the UCAS application.

1. **Personal information.** Your name, date of birth and gender.
2. **Contact and residency.** Your telephone number, postal and email address, your 'nominated access' and residency details. 'Nominated access' is someone who can act on your behalf if you are unavailable at any time during the application period. You need to read the instructions carefully to avoid making mistakes.
3. **Nationality.** Your nationality, questions about UK student visa, settled or pre-settled status in the UK, and your passport details.
4. **Supporting information.** Questions about you and your family living or working in the EU, EEA or Switzerland.
5. **English Language Skills.** Question on whether English is your first language; if it is not, you can submit your IELTS or TOEFL English proficiency test numbers.
6. **Student finance.** If you are planning to apply for student finance, you can complete this section to make your finance application easier. (UCAS will share your information, to make the two processes more streamlined.)

7. **More about you.** Declaration of any physical and/or mental health condition, long-term illness or learning difference.
8. **Education.** This means your examination results, where you have studied, and any examinations to be sat.
9. **Employment.** If you have had gaps in your education because you were in employment, you need to give the details here.
10. **Personal statement.** See Chapter 5 for more about this.
11. **Your choices of university.** You are allowed to choose five courses. Pay particular attention to the course codes and university codes, and ensure that all of the required information (where you intend to live, to which campus you are applying, etc.) is included.

Once you have completed all of these sections, your referee will add his or her comments about your suitability for your chosen courses, as well as your predicted grades. Your referee is normally someone at your school or college (such as a house-master or head of sixth form), but for applicants who are not at school, this might be an employer (see Chapter 7).

Suggested timescale

Here is a suggested timescale to help you fill in the UCAS application to the best of your ability.

Year 12

September onwards: Arrange some relevant work experience (if you haven't already), and start making your way through a focused reading list.

May/June: Do some serious thinking. Get ideas from friends, relatives, teachers, books, etc. If possible, visit some campuses before you go away anywhere during the summer.

June/July: Make a shortlist of your courses.

August: Get your hands on some copies of the official and alternative (student-written) prospectuses, and departmental brochures for extra detail. They can usually be found in school or college libraries, but all the information can also be found by looking at university websites. Write a first draft of your personal statement over the summer holidays.

Year 13

September: Complete your application online and submit it to UCAS via a referee. Your referee will write a reference outlining all the major reasons why a university should accept you as a candidate. It will be a positive interpretation of your qualities. It will be a significant factor in the relative success of your UCAS application.

16 October: Deadline for applying for places at Oxford or Cambridge and applications to study Medicine, Dentistry and Veterinary Science.

November: Universities hold their open days and sometimes interviews. Entrance examinations for some Oxford and Cambridge courses.

31 January: Deadline for submitting your application to UCAS. (Late applications may be considered, but your chances are limited since some of the places will have already gone.)

February: Universities begin to make their decisions and offers will be sent directly to you. If you are rejected by all of your choices, you can use UCAS Extra (opens 23 February) to look at other universities. Some universities make offers earlier than this.

18 May: You must tell UCAS which offer you have accepted firmly and which one is your backup if you receive all your university decisions by 8 June. If you receive all decisions by 12 July, you must reply to all offers by 17 July (including Extra choices). If you decide to change your mind about your offers and had only accepted them in the previous 14 days, you can contact UCAS to make changes to your initial decision.

Spring/Summer: Fill out yet more forms – this time for fees and student loans. You can get these from your school, college or local authority.

Summer: Sit your exams and wait for your results. If you are sitting exams in the UK (e.g. A level, Scottish Highers, International Baccalaureate), UCAS and your universities will receive your results automatically. When the results are published, UCAS will get in touch and tell you whether your chosen universities have confirmed your conditional offers. For a full list of qualifications that UCAS receives, see the UCAS website. If you are taking an examination that UCAS does not receive or you are sitting exams outside the UK, you may need to send your results to your universities yourself. If you are an international student, your universities may also require you to send evidence of your English language qualification, such as IELTS. Your school or college should be able to help you with this and the university admissions team can tell you what you need to do.

Do not be too disappointed if you have not got into your chosen institution; just get in touch with your school/college or careers office and wait until Clearing begins in early July; Clearing runs until mid-October, and during this three-month period all remaining places are filled.

Equally, candidates with unconditional offers who received better grades than they expected and now decide to change their university can release themselves into Clearing using the 'decline you place' button in their application (see Chapter 8).

Entrance examinations

If you are applying to Oxford or Cambridge universities, it is likely that you will have to sit an extra entrance examination. Details of these can be found in *Getting into Oxford & Cambridge* (Trotman Education). The London School of Economics (LSE) also sets an entrance test, the Undergraduate Admissions Assessment (UGAA), for some candidates whose educational background is non-standard. The UGAA is an invitation test – you will be asked to sit the test if they believe you are a viable candidate. Other universities may be introducing extra tests in the future, and you should check on the UCAS website or with the university to find out whether you will need to sit one. These tests are used to further differentiate between students, as predicted A level grades are often not enough to separate candidates. A serious candidate would make sure they visit the appropriate website to ensure that they are prepared and know what to expect.

These entrance tests are designed to help admissions tutors decide whether applicants have the necessary aptitude for success in their chosen field. Here they are looking at ability and reasoning skills rather than your ability to do well in exams. The tests will look at your problem-solving, reasoning and critical-thinking skills and your ability to communicate your ideas in an organised, concise way in the extended answer sections.

TSA (Thinking Skills Assessment) Oxford

The TSA is required by Oxford if you take Economics and Management or Philosophy, Politics and Economics (PPE).

- This 2-hour pre-interview test is taken on 18 October; students will need to be registered (this should be done by your school or college) for the test by 29 September; the results are released in early January.
- It consists of 50 multiple-choice questions to be completed in 90 minutes and a 30-minute essay from a choice of four questions.
- Details and practice papers can be found at www.admissions testing.org/for-test-takers/thinking-skills-assessment/tsa-oxford/preparing-for-tsa-oxford.

Sample question and answer from TSA Section 1, 2021

The fairy lights on a Christmas tree are in three colours, blue, green and silver. The blue lights flash every 5 seconds, the green lights flash every 8 seconds and the silver lights flash every 12 seconds. The lights have all just flashed at the same time. How many times will they all flash at the same time in the next 45 minutes?

A 5
B 22
C 45
D 108
E 112

Source: www.admissionstesting.org/for-test-takers.
Reproduced with the kind permission of
Cambridge Assessment Admissions Testing.

Answer: B

NB: Autumn 2023 will be the last session of the TSA delivered by Cambridge Assessment Admission Testing (CAAT). Candidates should check the University of Oxford's website for details of latest testing arrangements.

Other Oxbridge admissions assessments

For 2024 entry, most students who apply for Economics at Cambridge will be required to sit a pre-interview written assessment – the Test of Mathematics for University Admission (TMUA), which assesses mathematical thinking and reasoning skills.

However, as stated on the Cambridge Assessment website (www.admissionstesting.org/news/view/reforms-to-cambridge-assessment-admissions-testing-from-2024) CAAT is to withdraw from delivering the TMUA with effect from 2025 entry, alongside other Cambridge and Oxford admission tests. Candidates should check the latest entry requirements directly on the Cambridge and Oxford university websites.

LSE UGAA

- Candidates are informed at the beginning of March in the academic year of application if they are required to sit the UG Admissions Assessment (UGAA).
- It consists of a three-hour written paper in two sections: an essay question and mathematical knowledge.
- Details and practice papers can be found at www.lse.ac.uk/study-at-lse/Undergraduate/Prospective-Students/How-to-Apply/UGAA.

Other university and college admissions tests

Other universities and colleges that set admissions tests for business, economics and related courses include:

- Bedford College (Business)
- Birkbeck (Accounting; Accounting and Management with Finance;

Accounting and Management; Business; Business Psychology; Economic and Social Policy; Financial Economics; Management)
- Birmingham Metropolitan College (Business)
- Lancaster University (Accounting, Auditing and Finance)
- Pearson College (Business Management; Business Management with Finance; Business Management with Global Industries; Business Management with Law; Business Management and Entrepreneurship; Business Management with Marketing)
- University of Westminster (Fashion Merchandise Management).

For more details, visit www.ucas.com/undergraduate/applying-university/admissions-tests.

Taking a gap year

Most admissions tutors are happy for students to take a gap year in between their final year at school or college and the start of university. Of course, whether or not your gap year enhances and strengthens your application depends on what your gapyear plans entail.

There are two application routes for students taking gap years. One option is for students to apply for deferred entry – that is, applying in the final year of the A level course for entry a year later. So, a student sitting A levels in June 2023 would apply for entry in September/October 2024, not 2023. Alternatively, students can apply at the start of the gap year, once their A level results are known. There are advantages in both routes, depending on your plans and A level grades.

Deferred entry

With deferred entry:

- you will know where you are going to study in August, before you start your gap year
- you will not need to interrupt your gap year plans for interviews
- if you are unsuccessful in getting offers from your chosen universities or courses, you can reapply during the gap year.

Applying during the gap year

If you apply during the gap year:

- you will know your examination grades, so you can target your application much more effectively
- if your school is not predicting high grades but you feel confident in achieving higher than the predictions, you do not run the risk of being rejected based on the predictions.

Whichever route you take, it is important to plan the gap year properly so that it is clear to the universities that you (and they) will benefit from it.

The point of the gap year is to gain work or life experience, maturity and independence, or to earn money to help fund your studies. Admissions tutors are not going to be impressed with a gap year that involves watching TV and sleeping simply because you worked hard at your A levels and feel like a break from study.

Here is an excerpt from a personal statement:

'I am going to take a gap year during which I hope to travel and to gain more work experience.'

This is not going to convince the admissions tutors that (a) you have actually made any plans at all, or (b) this is a year that is likely to help you develop or bring new skills and ideas on to their courses.

A better version might be:

'During my gap year, I have arranged a placement with a local travel agent, where I will be assisting with planning group tours to various European countries. I hope that this will help me to understand more about how a company sets its prices and its budgets, particularly in a field where prices and exchange rates fluctuate on a day-to-day basis. The work experience will also be useful because, from March, I will be travelling in Asia, visiting India, Thailand, Vietnam and Cambodia. In Cambodia, I have arranged to teach English in an orphanage for one month. To fund this, I will be working in the evenings in a local restaurant while on my work placement with the travel company.'

This is much more impressive because the candidate has linked what she will do to her future degree course (business studies), and it is clear that she has thought carefully about what she will do during the year.

Students often use phrases such as 'I hope to ...' when 'I have arranged ...' or 'I have planned ...' are more likely to convince the university selectors that they are going to use the year usefully.

Gap year plans

Gap year plans do not have to involve travel to distant countries (although this is a useful and enjoyable thing to do). There are many other fulfilling ways of using your 12 months. The important thing is to be able to justify the plans either at the interview or in your personal statement. Other things you might consider include:

- internships (see Chapter 2)
- full- or part-time employment to earn money or to gain experience
- full- or part-time courses, such as IT, art, languages or practical skills
- helping with a university research project

- voluntary or charity work
- community projects.

If you are not sure whether your chosen university will be happy for you to take a gap year, contact it at the start of your final year of A levels and ask. Many university websites include details of their gap year policy.

Replies from the universities

After your application has been assessed by the university, you will receive a response. You can also follow the progress of your application using the online UCAS Hub facility. You will receive one of three possible responses from each university:

1. a conditional offer
2. an unconditional offer
3. a rejection.

If you receive a conditional offer, you will be told what you need to achieve in your A levels. This could be in grade terms, for example AAB (and the university might specify a particular grade in a particular subject – AAB with an A in economics), or in UCAS Tariff points (for example 120 points from three A levels – see Chapter 3). Unconditional offers are offers for which students have already met the entry requirements. Perhaps the student has already sat their A levels, e.g. a gap year student who applies after receiving their results; or perhaps the university has decided the student's results won't affect whether or not they are accepted. A 'conditional unconditional' is an offer that is only unconditional if the student selects that university as their Firm choice. Such offers are expected to be less common in 2023/24 due to criticism of them by the UK government. Rejection means that you have been unsuccessful in your application to that university.

If you receive five rejections, then you can enter the UCAS Extra scheme, through which you can make one additional choice at a time; this service is free and is open between 23 February and 4 July. You may also use UCAS Extra if you change your mind about the courses you have applied for and you decline all the offers you are holding. Be careful when doing this: read the information in Chapter 8 on using UCAS Extra.

Once you have received responses from all five universities, you will need to make your choice of the university offer you wish to accept. This is called your firm choice. You can also choose an insurance offer, which is effectively a second choice with a lower grade requirement. UCAS will give you a deadline of about a month to make this decision from the date when you receive your fifth response. You may have a different deadline to your friends, so make sure you know what your own deadline is by checking UCAS Hub.

5 | The personal statement

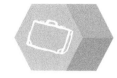

Currently, the most important part of the UCAS application is the personal statement as it gives you, the applicant, the space to have your voice heard.

However, recently UCAS have shared findings from studies carried out as part of the 'Reimagining UK Admissions' report (www.ucas.com/about-us/news-and-insights/reforming-admissions), and the personal statement is one of the areas that is being closely looked at. It is expected to undergo some significant changes in the near future, and students are strongly advised to check the information for the most up to date information.

The 'Future of Undergraduate Admissions' report, published in January 2023, highlights that 83% of students found the process of writing a personal statement stressful, and 79% found it very challenging to complete without support. As a result, UCAS have tested various new models that could improve on the current approach, and identified a preference for structured questions in six key areas, currently as follows:

- Motivation for course – what are your reasons for studying your chosen course?
- Preparedness for course – how will your current or previous studies help you to succeed in your degree?
- Preparation through other experiences (e.g. work experience or volunteering) – why are these useful?
- Extenuating circumstances – is there anything that the universities and colleges need to know about, to help them put your achievements and experiences so far into context?
- Preparedness for study – what have you done to prepare yourself for university life?
- Preferred learning styles – talk about your learning and assessment styles, and how your course choices match that.

Any changes to the format of the Personal Statement will be introduced no earlier than the 2024 application cycle (for entry onto courses in 2025). However, for now, the personal statement is where you have 47 lines (or 4,000 characters including spaces, whichever you use first) to convince the five universities you are applying to that:

- you are serious about wanting to study on the course
- you have researched the options available to you for the degree course and for your future career
- you are suitable for the course
- you are a well-rounded individual who can contribute to the life of the university.

> 'Before you apply, look at the university requirements. Due to the mathematics and statistics included in an economics degree, many universities specify a certain minimum grade at GCSE Mathematics and some require A level Mathematics. At a small number, further mathematics may be desirable. A level Economics is not essential; studying both economics and business studies should, as a rule, be avoided. In some cases, candidates offering three A levels which include further mathematics may be disadvantaged, as this will be expected as a fourth A level and may not count towards offers. Check the requirements of each university carefully if in doubt.'
>
> An admissions tutor for Economics

Before you start to write your personal statement, you need to finalise your choice of courses. Why? Because the personal statement has to convince an admissions tutor at a university that you are a serious applicant. It is important to remember that you write one personal statement that is read by all five universities to which you are applying. The people reading the personal statement do not know which other universities you are applying to, or for what courses. All they will be assessing is whether your personal statement is applicable for their particular course.

If an admissions tutor is selecting students for an economics degree course, he or she will be looking for personal statements that address economics; if an admissions tutor is selecting students to study business studies, he or she will be expecting to read about business-related issues. It is important, therefore, to ensure that there is as much compatibility between your five choices as possible, otherwise you run the risk of being rejected by all of them.

> 'To study management, you need to demonstrate that you are capable of managing yourself. Your personal statement needs to be structured, organised and free of spelling or grammatical errors. You should aim to be unique and original and provide a good opening line that reveals something about your aptitude and enthusiasm. I really like to see statements that demonstrate

personality and flair but don't go too over the top. Keep it formal and remain objective. I am impressed by applicants who describe situations where they've demonstrated relevant skills like good communication or teamwork, problem-solving, initiative, leadership or achieving goals.'

Admissions tutor, University Campus, Suffolk

Here are some examples of the opening paragraphs of personal statements by MPW students who gained places to study business and economics.

In the pursuit of my business ambition I am looking to join an academic institute that tailors its courses to the ever-changing economic and commercial climate. I am confident that your university will provide me with the solid foundations needed to acquire the analytical and financial skills to prosper in the global commercial environment. I hold a genuine desire to study and would love the opportunity to continue my development to degree and masters level.

Business Management, King's College London

This is a simple and clear outline of the reasons why the student wants to study for a degree – to increase their chances of success for future business ventures. There is no shame in stating you want to manage your own business and enjoy commercial success.

I aspire to work in fashion industry, a fast-changing environment, that would allow me to make a mark by applying my knowledge and practical skills acquired. I would relish the opportunity of studying fashion management to experiment with new ideas, delve deeper into the challenges this industry poses and consider how these evolve within contemporary culture. I see your academic centre of excellence as the perfect platform for me to unlock my full potential and realise these ambitions.

Fashion Management, University of the Arts London

This is a good example of clearly expressed future goals and a wish to make a mark in a specific industry.

Studying Economics has informed my understanding of world events as well as changing my perception of global business. Macroeconomics most appeals to me, especially the difficulties in handling conflicting objectives. I am particularly interested in the challenge of interpreting statistics over time given the inability to control variables in the real world.

Issues such as inequality and economic stability underpin all political arguments, from the EU referendum to sustainable development of the third world. Another area that fascinates me is how policy decisions taken to incentivise the population to behave in a certain way sometimes have unintended consequences which distort markets.

Economics, University of Bristol

This statement shows a clear understanding of the key features of macroeconomics. It is fine to highlight only one aspect of a subject. It does not undermine the case for you studying the entire subject as a degree. Also, the applicant has linked their academic interest to current political and economic developments. Admissions tutors will be impressed by applicants who discuss relevant issues outside their specific discipline.

My initial interest in finance was developed through the IFS Student Investor Challenge, which stimulated my investment in the Chinese stock market. Differences in decision-making techniques used between virtual and actual stock exchange, have led to my realisation of the impact of government intervention and the changing patterns of the market. As a result, I am currently reading politics, international relations and economics for my foundation course, in order to consolidate my previous knowledge, as well as to further investigate the application of these strongly-related disciplines on real world financial status.

Finance and Accounting, City University

This student outlines the origins of their interest in the subject. There is no disadvantage in explaining a recent development – no one will believe you if you claim you wanted to study finance and accounting since you were a small child. Also, the applicant has linked their current subjects to their chosen course, showing they are both aware of the academic challenges of their chosen degree and they are prepared to undertake their chosen course.

Applying for more than one course at the same university?

The UCAS system allows you to apply for more than one course at a particular university. But beware: applying for two courses at the same institution does not double your chances of studying there. The key point to consider is that the admissions tutors for the two departments at the same university will know you have applied to another department in the university. The courses must be adjacent disciplines, so you should not be applying for Business and English Literature at the same university.

This may appear strange, but university admissions tutors are not impressed by students who appear to be particularly keen to study at their university. The key issue is the course, not where you wish to study. The harsh reality is admissions tutors will presume you have non-academic reasons for wishing to study at their university (close to home, close to family members, close to your favourite football team, the same university as your mates or your girl/boyfriend). None of these considerations makes you an attractive candidate for admissions tutors.

Applying for two different courses on your application is fine, but no more than two adjacent courses is advisable. You can apply for a history and economics combined course, a history course and an economics course with a personal statement equally dedicated to history and economics. Admissions tutors know students apply for other courses, and they will appreciate the value of combined degrees, even if they do not offer the combination. However, a third subject in your personal statement will significantly dilute your application.

So bear the following in mind.

- **Rule Number 4**. When writing the personal statement, try to imagine how it will come across to each of the departments to which you are applying. Don't try to write something too general just so you have the luxury of applying to a wider range of courses.

The structure of the personal statement

There is no one formula for a perfect personal statement. It is called a personal statement because it should reflect your interests and achievements. However, as a general guideline, the personal statement should cover four areas:

1. why you have chosen the course
2. how you have investigated whether the course is suitable for you
3. what makes you stand out from your peers
4. other information relevant to the application; for example, if you are taking a gap year, what you will be doing during that year.

Why you have chosen the course

This could include:

- what first interested you in economics, business or management; for example, watching the news about the failure of a bank, an article on the impact of the Covid-19 pandemic on the global economy, or personal experience, such as work experience or the family business
- a particular career plan
- a combination of your particular interests and academic skills.

How you have investigated whether the course is suitable for you

This could include:

- books, periodicals or websites that you have read
- work experience (see Chapter 2)
- lectures that you have attended
- skills that you have gained from your A levels.

What makes you stand out from your peers

This could include:

- academic achievements; for example, prizes or awards
- extracurricular activities and achievements
- relevant work experience
- responsibilities; for example as school prefect, head of house, captain of netball team, or voluntary or charity work
- evidence of teamwork; for example, sports teams, Duke of Edinburgh Award expeditions, or part-time jobs
- travel.

Other information relevant to the application

This could include:

- gap year plans
- personal circumstances; for example, it might be necessary for you to study in your home city because of the need to help care for a family member.

'This is not the place to list your A levels and what you've done in them. It is also not the place to try and link everything to economics, especially if the link is tenuous. Try and avoid saying

"Studying English literature has improved my essay writing skills and helped me construct concise arguments/mathematics has helped with my data analysis skills". These will be pretty self-evident and a waste of characters. Instead, talk about what in your A levels (related to economics) has interested you and why. If you found it particularly interesting, you may want to briefly talk about any studies that you did during A level Economics or subjects that particularly interested you. Don't just explain what different areas of economics are about – reflect on them. Admissions tutors will be familiar with the concepts you're talking about. While you want to present yourself as a good economics student, if your personal statement becomes simply a short essay about economics or a particular theory or concept then it's saying nothing about you as a person.'

An admissions tutor for Economics

Sample personal statement 1 (character count: 1,605)

I have chosen to study management at university because I want to run a business in the future, and management skills will be very important for this. I first became interested in management because my father runs a company and so I was able to see how important this aspect of the business is.

Last summer, I spent two weeks shadowing a department manager in a local company, and I gained an insight into the skills required to be a successful manager. In particular, I observed the need for good communication skills. I enjoy reading *The Economist* and the business sections of the national newspapers.

I am studying mathematics, economics and physics at A level. Mathematics is useful because it helps me to understand balance sheets and share prices, which are essential skills for a successful businessman. Economics has taught me how a company's success depends on how it adapts to the way the market is performing, and how it copes with fluctuations in the global economy. Physics teaches me how to be analytical and how to solve problems.

At school, I am captain of the 1st XV rugby team. This requires the ability to show leadership qualities and to manage people. It also allows me to get rid of stress. I play the trombone in the school orchestra, which involves teamwork and manual dexterity. I like reading, going to the cinema, and photography. I also have a passion for opera. On Saturdays, I work at the local Louisiana

> Fried Turkey fast-food restaurant, and so I have gained excellent communication and teamwork skills. In my gap year I hope to travel and to gain more work experience.

Points raised by sample personal statement 1

- It is too short, at fewer than 2,000 characters (remember the maximum is 4,000 characters). You should aim to use the full amount of space available.
- Although the candidate has addressed all of the relevant issues, there is a lack of detail. It is too general and tells us very little about the candidate.
- It is not very personal.

An admissions tutor's comments on sample personal statement 1

'I have chosen to study management at university because I want to run a business in the future, and management skills will be very important for this.' (1) *'I first became interested in management because my father runs a company'* (2) *'and so I was able to see how important this aspect of the business is.'* (3)

1. Why are management skills important? Give an example of a situation you have seen, discussed or read about that illustrates this.
2. Give details of the company – what does it do? Who does it trade with?
3. An example would add detail to this section – perhaps recount an incident that shows the importance of a good management structure, or about the need to delegate.

'Last summer, I spent two weeks shadowing a department manager' (4) *'in a local company,'* *'and I gained an insight into the skills required to be a successful manager. In particular, I observed the need for good communication skills.'* (5) *'I enjoy reading* The Economist *and the business sections of the national newspapers.'* (6)

4. Which department? What did the company do? How big was it? You could write something along the lines of '… which manufactured electric motors to be used in agricultural settings …' This might well stimulate an interesting discussion at the interview stage.
5. Give an example, such as 'As an example of this, I remember one occasion when a local farmer needed us to adapt one of the products to …'

6. Also, give an example that relates to something you have studied at A level. This should be the strongest and longest section of the personal statement. I want to know much more about what the applicant gained from the work experience and why it has convinced him/her that my course is the right one.

'I am studying mathematics, economics and physics at A level. Mathematics is useful because it helps me to understand balance sheets and share prices, which are essential skills for a successful businessman. Economics has taught me how a company's success depends on how it adapts to the way the market is performing, and how it copes with fluctuations in the global economy. Physics teaches me how to be analytical and how to solve problems.' (7)

7. This is OK, but could do with links between what the applicant has studied at A level and what he/she has discovered about business and management in the real world through reading and work experience.

'At school, I am captain of the 1st XV rugby team. This requires the ability to show leadership qualities and to manage people. It also allows me to get rid of stress. I play the trombone in the school orchestra, which involves teamwork and manual dexterity. I like reading, going to the cinema, and photography. I also have a passion for opera. On Saturdays, I work at the local Louisiana Fried Turkey fast-food restaurant, and so I have gained excellent communication and teamwork skills. In my gap year I hope to travel and to gain more work experience.' (8)

8. This sentence could be more detailed – rather than 'hope to travel', I would like to see something more definite – 'I have arranged to ...' I want to be reassured that the applicant is going to use the gap year wisely and to benefit from it.

Adding the extra information requested by this admissions tutor would add detail, make it more interesting for him to read (so he is more likely to want to meet the student), demonstrate that the student is interested enough in the subject to be thinking about links between his studies and his experiences, and bring the statement up to the required length.

So remember the following.

- **Rule Number 5.** Details turn an easily forgettable personal statement into something that will stand out from the rest.

Links and connections

As you will have noticed from the previous example, a good way to show that you have thought about the subject and the course is to make links and connections between your different areas of research and preparation. You could think about linking:

- aspects of your A level subjects with aspects of the course
- qualities necessary for success in this field with your own experiences; for example, captaining a school team or organising a school event
- an article that you read with something that you observed in your work experience.

You could start this process by making lists, or diagrammatically, as in Figure 2.

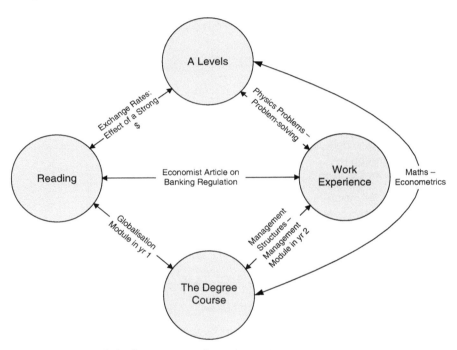

Figure 2 Making links between study and experience

How to get started on the personal statement

How not to get started on your personal statement would be to …

- plan how you are going to say all you want in exactly 47 lines
- write down your ideas in perfectly formed sentences, suitable for the final version
- download sample personal statements from the internet and try to adapt them.

A better strategy is to start by making lists of anything that you think is relevant to your application, then to begin organising them into sections. Your personal statement could include some of the following points.

'My interest in the subject began because of ...

- a newspaper article I read
- a book I read
- a news item
- my work experience
- my parents' work
- my A level subjects.'

'I have researched this subject by ...

- reading books
- reading the *Financial Times*
- reading *The Economist*
- reading *Business Week*
- work experience
- attending lectures
- talking to ...
- downloading a podcast of a university lecture.'

'My work experience taught me ...

- that the qualities a good manager/accountant/businessman/ economist needs are ...
- how to relate what I have been taught in A level economics to real-life situations ...
- the importance of teamwork/accuracy/decision making ...'

Other relevant points are given below.

- 'My A level subjects are useful because ...'
- 'My Saturday job is useful because ...'
- 'My role as school prefect has taught me ...'
- 'Being captain of the 1st XV (or netball, or leader of the orchestra, or ...) has taught me ...'
- 'During my gap year I have arranged to ...'
- 'I was awarded first prize for ...'

Only when you have the ideas structured into some sort of logical order should you start to write full sentences and to link the points. Which leads to the next rule.

- **Rule Number 6**. Always use examples and evidence to illustrate the points you are making in the personal statement.

Language

Given the limit on the number of characters (4,000) that make up the personal statement, it is important to make every sentence count, and not to waste space with passages that are at best too general and at worst meaningless. You should use clear, simple English and make sure that the content of what you are writing impresses the selectors, rather than trying to win them over with flowery, overcomplicated phrases.

> *'I was privileged to be able to undertake some work experience with a well-known high-street bank where I was able to see the benefit of having the ability to be confident with information technology.'*
> **– 199 characters**

This could be rewritten as:

> *'My three weeks' work placement at HSBC showed me the importance of being proficient in using spreadsheets.'*
> **– 106 characters**

Similarly:

> *'I was honoured to be able to captain my school Under-14, Under-15, Second XV and First XV rugby sides, and from this I learnt how to be an effective leader and an excellent communicator.'*
> **– 186 characters**

… could be rewritten as:

> *'Captaining my school 1st XV taught me the importance of strong leadership and communication skills.'*
> **– 99 characters**

Phrases to avoid include the following.

- 'I was honoured to be …'
- 'I was privileged to …'
- 'From an early age …'
- 'It has always been my dream to …'

Hence …

- **Rule Number 7**. Every word counts, so do not waste space by using overcomplicated language or words that are designed to impress.

Sample personal statement 2 was written by an international student who was subsequently offered an interview from Cambridge and received several offers from his chosen universities. It is very individual in style, and reflects the student's interest in the impacts of the pandemic as well as other factors on developing countries.

Sample personal statement 2 (character count: 3,372)

The recent global pandemic reveals the inequality prevalent in a global society – competition between countries to get a limited supply of vaccines led to troublesome polarity, in which rich countries have control of developing, manufacturing and distributing the vaccines, while poor countries have trouble accessing them except through international institutions (such as WHO) for humanitarian purposes. What intrigued me most was that the countries that rely on voluntary donations of vaccines were the same poor countries 20 years ago. While the Korean economy successfully experienced economic development from the 1960s, differentiating itself from its fellow poor countries, the recent pandemic confirmed to me that poor countries tend to remain poor while rich countries tend to become wealthier.

Having been a rigorous reader of *The Economist*, I looked at every article on developing countries from the early 2000s. In my opinion, the first step to taking inter-country inequality seriously is to acknowledge that in economics, competition need not be a zero-sum game. As the increasing volume of trade proves, both developing and developed countries can be better off than the state of self-sufficiency. However, *Bad Samaritans*, by Ha-Joon Chang, confirmed to me that there is an unequal playing field of competition between developed and developing countries. For instance, despite the fact that the advanced economies are where they are through fossil-fuel-driven industrialisation, it is harsh to now put the environmental responsibility on developing countries and ask them to share more burden. Furthermore, *Gambling on Development* by Stefan Dercon warned that developing countries mostly fail to establish a good education and healthcare system, thus preventing the benefits of trade from being sustainable. This research convinced me that free trade is not a sufficient condition for long-term prosperity, and government intervention is needed to prepare the economy to be internationally competitive.

Working as an intern in a hospital in Korea broadened my insight as to why the role of government is important for long-term prosperity. Universal health insurance, and mandatory medical insurance for employees and their dependents improved labour productivity. And investing in higher education institutions led to a large pool of engineers and programmers in the Korean labour market. However, from attending a public lecture by the Korean Economic Association, I learned that developed countries also face problems like de-industrialisation, an aging society, and a widening trade deficit with developing countries such as China, and Korea is no exception to these problems. It is the government's role to tackle these issues. However, in my opinion, the problem is that government does not have perfect information, and can distort incentives, resulting in regulatory capture and tax evasion. This could lead to a worse-off situation than free-market allocation.

The reason why economics fascinates me is that every theme is subject to pros and cons – it investigates human behaviour at an individual or aggregate level in which many different factors affect the decision-making process. So how can an economist conclude which factor has the strongest explanatory power? From an online public lecture on Introductory Economics, I learned that economists rely on statistical techniques to make quantitative support to qualitative statements. Appreciating such data analytics resided in economics persuaded me to study Further Mathematics at A level. In school debate club, I try to make my arguments more robust with data references. In school rugby competitions, I enjoyed applying statistics and probability to determine the best scenario for winning.

Overall, I want to study economics because it will provide me with the best foundation upon which I can appreciate complex real-world problems and provide solutions to them.

General tips

- Before submitting your application, ensure you checked it through very carefully for careless errors. Print a copy out to read through; it is harder to identify potential errors on a screen.
- A teacher or parent should read your personal statement before submitting to ensure no errors slip through.
- Keep a copy of your personal statement so that you can remind yourself of what you have said, should you be called for interview.

And remember the seven rules for a successful application.

1. Research the course content.
2. Research the entrance requirements.
3. Find out your grade predictions.
4. Ensure your personal statement focuses on the course but remember to imagine how it will come across to each of the departments to which you are applying.
5. Include enough detail in the personal statement to make it stand out.
6. Illustrate your points with examples and evidence.
7. Every word in a personal statement counts, so don't use complicated language just to impress the admissions tutor.

6 | Succeeding at interview

Some universities will want to interview prospective students before making their final decisions (Oxford and Cambridge will always interview before offering a place). Post-pandemic, some universities, including Oxbridge, are still offering interviews online.

Interviews need not be as daunting as you fear. They are designed to help the people asking the questions to find out as much about you as they can. Treat the experience positively as a chance to put yourself across well, rather than as an obstacle course designed to catch you out.

If you are invited for an interview, here are some points to bear in mind.

- Remember that if you shine in your interview and impress the admissions staff, they may drop their grades slightly and make you a lower offer.
- Make eye contact and use confident body language.
- Interviewers are more interested in what you know than what you do not. If you are asked a question you do not know the answer to, say so. Waffling simply wastes time and lets you down. To lie, of course, is even worse – especially for anyone hoping to demonstrate the integrity and honesty suited to a business career.
- Remember: your future tutor might be among the people interviewing you, so it's important to be polite.
- Enthusiasm, a strong commitment to your subject and, above all, a willingness to learn are extremely important attitudes to convey.
- An ability to think on your feet is vital … another prerequisite for a career in business or management. Pre-learned answers never work. Putting forward an answer using examples and factual knowledge to reinforce your points will impress interviewers far more. Essential preparation includes revision of the personal statement on your UCAS application, so do not include anything in your UCAS application that you are not prepared to speak about at interview.
- Questions may well be asked about your extracurricular activities. This is often a tactic designed to put you at your ease and to find out about the sort of person you are; therefore, your answers should be thorough and enthusiastic.
- At the end of the interview, you will probably be asked whether there is anything you would like to ask your interviewer. If you have nothing to ask, then say that your interview has covered everything

you thought of. It is sensible, however, to have up your sleeve one or two questions of a serious kind – to do with the course, the tuition and so on. However, it is not wise to ask anything that you could and should have found out from the prospectus, such as 'what accommodation do you offer to first-year students?'

- Above all, end on a positive note, and remember to smile! Make them remember you when they review their list of 20 or more candidates at the end of the day.

Preparation for an interview

Preparation for an interview should be an intensification of the work you are already doing outside class for your A level courses. Interviewers will be looking for evidence of an academic interest and commitment that extends beyond the classroom. They will also be looking for an ability to apply the theories and methods that you have been learning in your A level courses to the real world.

Whichever resources you use, this advice assumes that you will be taking a single honours business, management or economics degree, but if you have chosen a joint or combined honours course you will have to prepare yourself for questions on those other subjects as well.

Either way, the interview is a chance for you to demonstrate knowledge of, commitment to and enthusiasm for your chosen discipline. The only way to do this is to be extremely well informed. Interviewers will want to know your reasons for wishing to study business. It is important to be aware of the many aspects of business, e.g. marketing, finance, personnel, and be clear about the differences between the various functions.

Newspapers and magazines

As an A level student, you should already be reading a quality newspaper every day. Before your interview, it is vital that you are aware of current affairs related to the course for which you are being interviewed. the *Financial Times* will give you a good grasp of business, as will reading the business sections of other newspapers (not tabloids). The 'Markets' section of the *Financial Times* will give you an overview of current interest rates, inflation rates and equity index values. You should also keep up to date with current affairs in general.

Magazines are another important source of comment on current issues and deeper analysis. *The Economist* is a popular example, but you might also find it helpful to pick up a more specialist magazine such as *Talk Business*. Reading professionally written articles keeps you well informed about current events and gives you the chance to see how the vocabulary and language of business are used to communicate news and views.

Magazines such as *Enterprise* and *HR* could also have some articles of interest to you. You do not have to buy all these – visit public libraries and your school library and/or use the web to keep up to date with the business press. There are also subject-specific magazines such as Hodder Education's *Review* series, based around A level study. The interviewer does not have to have read the article, but you can show you are 'reading around the subject' which is a key feature of the more able students.

Television, film and radio

It is also important to watch or listen to the news every day, again paying particular attention to business and economic news. Documentaries and programmes about the economy, business ventures, the politics of business and so on can be enormously helpful in showing how what you are studying is applied to actual situations and events. *Panorama* is a good example of the sort of television programme it would be useful to watch. *Dragons' Den* is also quite informative for those students particularly interested in entrepreneurship. *Inside Job* is an American documentary film which details the events leading up to the global financial crisis of 2008 and reveals the systemic corruption of the financial services industry. Finally, *A Beautiful Mind* is an American biographical drama film based on a Nobel Laureate in Economics, John Nash, known for his work on game theory.

Radio 4 offers *Money Box*, while the *Today* programme in the morning has up-to-the-minute reporting on economic and business developments, often with interviews with those most closely involved. The Times radio station is also a good source of news and analysis. Finally, it is also a good idea to know the names of the chairman of the Confederation of British Industry (CBI) and the governor of the Bank of England, for example, along with the names of the country's top businesspeople. You can make a point of listening to what they have to say when they appear on *Question Time* or *Newsnight* on television, or *Any Questions* on Radio 4.

Podcasts

The last few years have seen incredible growth in the podcast market, and podcasts increasingly serve as a convenient and accessible educational tool. Most news providers have their own podcast channel, which generally provide deeper analysis and commentary on a specific news story. 'The Daily', by the *New York Times*, creates engaging and informative podcasts which are usually between 30 minutes and 1 hour in length – great for a morning commute, walk to the shops or trip to the gym! 'Economist Radio' is a podcast produced by *The Economist* magazine and the 'FT News Briefing' provides a 'rundown of the most important global business stories you need to know for the coming day, from the newsroom of the *Financial Times*', and is available every weekday morning.

The internet

A wealth of easily accessible, continually updated and useful information is, of course, available on the internet. Given the ease with which information can be accessed, there is really no excuse for not being able to keep up to date with relevant current issues. Radio programmes can be downloaded as podcasts and listened to at times convenient to you; the BBC's iPlayer gives access to current affairs and documentary programmes after they have been broadcast; www.ted.com/talks is an online library of over 4,000 educational lectures; newspapers can be read online ... the list is endless. In this age of information overload, anyone who is serious about keeping abreast of current issues has unlimited opportunities to do so. Thus, an interviewer is not going to be impressed with a student who claims he or she has been too busy to know what is happening in his or her chosen areas of interest.

> **Case study**
>
> 'My first interview was a disaster. I had written about keeping up to date with current issues by reading *The Economist* and the second question they asked was about that week's edition. In fact, the last one I had read was three months before the interview. After that, they asked me about why I liked their course, and whether it differed in content from others I had applied for. What they really wanted to know was had I read their prospectus. I hadn't, and I got rejected.'
>
> Michael, on his interview for Economics

The interview

> 'An interview is an opportunity for the applicant to communicate one-to-one with a member of staff, to know more about the university and the course. When an applicant is genuinely enthusiastic about their subject, their confidence is evident. It is important to gather their thoughts about why they are doing the course, what they want to achieve and why they have chosen our university.
>
> 'We want to understand the applicant's motivation, suitability for the course and what they want to achieve through the course. We may also check the applicant's experience according to their application. In terms of preparation, it would be useful for applicants to think about questions they want to ask and ensure they write these down in advance.'
>
> A Business Studies admissions tutor, University of Reading

The interviewers want to know how *you* think, so that they can then decide whether you are 'teachable' and whether you would make a successful student on their course.

Interview questions are likely to test your knowledge of business and economics events and developments in the real world. Any relevant controversial topics could well be brought up by interviewers and you should be well informed enough to have an opinion about them from a business point of view.

It is important that your answers are delivered in appropriate language. You will impress interviewers with your fluent use of precise technical terms, so detailed knowledge of the definitions of words and phrases used in business and economics is essential.

You might be asked which part of your A level courses you have enjoyed most. You need to think carefully about this before interview and, if possible, steer the interview in the direction of these topics so you can display your knowledge.

Future plans and possible careers may also be discussed at interview. You will not be expected to have completely made up your mind about this, and, by the same token, you will not be held to what you say at interview after you have left university. Previous work experience is useful and you should be able to recall the precise tasks you carried out during your employment and think about them before interview so that you can answer questions on them fully and well. Questions of this kind will be asked to see whether you have an understanding of how business and management theories and methods are actually applied in the world outside school or college.

Interviewers will ask questions with a view to forming an opinion about the quality of your thought processes and your ability to negotiate. You may be presented with a real or supposed set of circumstances and then be asked to comment on their business implications.

As mentioned, current affairs are very likely to form a large part of the interview and could well be the basis for questions. An ability to see the opposite point of view while maintaining your own will mark you out as a strong business, economics or management degree candidate.

Do not forget that interview skills are greatly improved by practice. Talk through the issues outlined above with your friends and then arrange for a careers officer, teacher or family friend to give you a mock interview.

In any interview situation, it makes a better impression if you arrive in plenty of time for your interview and dress smartly and appropriately (people in business tend to look quite formal). Try to appear confident and enthusiastic in your interview – but listen carefully to the questions you are asked without interrupting, and always answer honestly.

Likely interview questions

Questions may be straightforward and specific, but they can range to the vague and border on the seemingly irrelevant as well. Be prepared for more than the obvious 'Why do you want to study management?' But remember, you wouldn't have been invited for interview unless you were a serious candidate for a place on the course, so be confident, and let your talents shine through. Many of the following questions could easily apply to both academic and work experience interviews. Try practising your answers to these.

Why have you chosen to study management?

Comment: Focus your answer to this question on how your studies and work experience have provided you with the motivation and interest to pursue this subject at university. This is an obvious starting point for your interviewers, and they will probably want you to expand on the reasons for choosing your course that you highlighted in your personal statement. Assume that this question will arise and practise your answer to it: ensure that what you say is well structured and that you do not waffle – try to keep your answer relatively short and certainly no longer than two minutes.

Why do you want to study at this university?

Comment: This is another standard opening question and one that you should certainly be prepared for. You could talk about why the location of the university appealed to you, or how you were attracted to it via a personal recommendation. A prime factor that distinguishes one institution from another is the course it offers. You will need to ensure that you have researched the course in some depth to see what is studied and how it is organised and structured.

Why have you chosen these A levels?

Comment: You may apply for university degree courses that differ significantly from your subjects at A level. This will require an explanation. It does not kill your application – you would not be attending an interview if they were not willing to offer you a place – but it is a question that requires an answer.

Have you visited here before?

Comment: If you have visited the university or attended an open day previously, this is your opportunity to mention it. Remember that the people conducting your interview will have contributed greatly to their department's open day and will welcome your feedback, but do keep it positive! Talk about it being a useful and informative occasion. Your interviewers will expect you to have done a lot of research into your chosen course and institution, so they will be expecting you to be well informed. (The university prospectuses and websites are good sources of information.) You do need to show that you are familiar with the particular institution to which you are applying. Answering this question by just saying 'No, but all universities are pretty much the same' will not improve your chances of getting a place.

What thoughts do you have on what you would like to do after you graduate?

Comment: Of course, you do not need to know exactly what career you would like to follow at the end of your degree at this stage – but you do need to have some thoughts on the kind of job you might be interested in. A possible answer might be: 'I would like a job that incorporates both my education and my practical skills: something combining my A level education with my working knowledge of customer service operations, entrepreneurial abilities and computer and administrative skills.' If, on the other hand, you do have a clear idea about what you would like to go into in the future, then talk about this – but remember to justify your reasons.

How do you think you are doing with your A levels?

Comment: The interviewer will know your predicted grades so you do not need to give too much information about these, but do state that you are working hard and making good progress. Talk about what topics you are studying at the moment and whether you are doing anything related to business and management. Elaborate on the aspects of the course you like, the skills you have gained and/or coursework projects where relevant. This is a relatively boring question, so take the opportunity to direct the conversation towards subjects that you are confident discussing and that will show you in the strongest light. Topics you are happy talking about should be prepared in advance.

What has attracted you to this course in particular?

Comment: This question, like the second one, enables you to show that you have thoroughly researched the particular course for which you are applying. You should draw on a particular aspect of the course that interests you and explain why. The university's website will generally give a precise breakdown of the core units that will be taught each year as well as the optional modules.

Tell me about any work experience you have had

Comment: This is an important question. Expand on the description of work experience that you gave in your personal statement. Do not just list the things you saw and did – mention how you felt about and reacted to what you were seeing and doing. Did you enjoy it? Was there anything that particularly interested or surprised you? Try to give as personal an account as possible.

What are the main things you learned from your work experience?

Comment: This is another standard question that follows naturally from the preceding one. Talk about the varied nature of your experience. There might have been things that surprised you about the functioning of a business or about new technology that was used. How did it differ from your expectations? You could try to link this with things that you have been taught at A level if you have taken business studies, economics or accounting. Work experience includes any part-time or weekend jobs that you might have done. The interviewer will understand that the main reason that you have your Saturday job in a clothes shop is to earn some extra money, but they will be interested in seeing whether you have learned anything from it that might be relevant to your future degree studies. There are many opportunities to do this. Take the example of the clothes shop – you could discuss:

- whether the shop is part of a nationwide chain, or whether it is an independent business – and the advantages and disadvantages of each
- how the shop advertises and markets its range of clothing
- who the target buyers are, and how the business targets them
- how the goods are priced, and who the main competitors are
- the managerial structure of the shop
- the effects of a recession or an economic boom (whichever is relevant at the time of your interview)
- where the clothes are made, and the implications of this for the UK's economy
- customer relations.

How do you keep up to date with current developments in economics?

Comment: Economics (and business and management) issues change every day and to demonstrate a genuine interest in these subjects requires you to keep up to date with current developments. You need to read quality newspapers on a daily basis, watch the news and read specialist websites.

Have you followed any business cases in the news recently?

Comment: As an A level student, you should be reading a newspaper (not a tabloid) every day. Talk about a recent article you have read and why you found it particularly interesting. This is another standard question and it is vital that you prepare your answer in advance. If you try to think of a topic off the top of your head without having given it any serious consideration previously, you could find that you are out of your depth if you have to deal with further questions on the subject.

Have you spoken to any people in business about their work? Have you visited any businesses?

Comment: Talk about people who work in business and what they have told you, and why you have found what they said interesting or motivating. When discussing a business that you have visited, give a different example from the one that you talked about in relation to your work experience. Mention what you learned about the workings of this business and how it operates.

In your personal statement you talked about 'X'. Can you please expand a bit on the statement you made about 'Y'?

Comment: Always re-read your personal statement! You were limited by how much you could write in there so must have carefully included your best ideas. Be prepared to be questioned on what you wrote and how you think. Ensure that you're confident with the topics you've referenced and that you can support your statements robustly. Practise talking out loud and in detail about things that you mentioned in your statement; ask your family and friends to question you on what you wrote. You should sound confident and ready to back up your ideas. Also, be prepared be challenged by interviewers on some of your arguments – this is their attempt to collect more information about how you think, and it is your opportunity to demonstrate your critical thinking skills and ability to think on your feet.

Other possible questions

Opposite are a selection of questions that have been asked in university interviews. You can use these as a basis for a mock interview. Ask someone who does not know you very well to ask you a selection of relevant questions from the list, and then ask them to assess how convincing your answers are. If there are areas that are obviously in need of work, then you can research in preparation for the real interview. However, do not try to learn 'right' answers to all of these questions and then recite them parrot fashion at the interview. If you do this you will come across as having obviously prepared your answers. There is also a danger that you will try to twist a question to suit one of your prepared answers, and you will appear evasive to the interviewer.

- What areas of business are you interested in?
- How does economics affect your daily life?
- What makes a good businessperson or manager?
- Can you give me a quick summary of the underlying reasons for the global financial crisis?
- Why do businesses fail?
- What is meant by 'marketing'?
- Why do share prices fluctuate?
- If you had £10million to invest in equities, where would you invest, and why?
- Is it a good thing that the Bank of England sets interest rates in the UK?
- What does it mean to be 'too big to fail', with reference to financial institutions?
- What is microeconomics?
- What is macroeconomics?
- What is globalisation?
- What is the current Bank of England base rate? And what is the current Federal Funds rate?
- Is globalisation a good thing?
- Who has responsibility for reducing global warming? Businesses or governments?
- Which sectors of the economy has the Covid-19 pandemic had the biggest impact on, and why?
- What do you know about David Ricardo, Friedrich Hayek and Adam Smith?
- Is the Chinese model of capitalism discredited?
- Has Brexit had an impact on global trade?
- Is there likely to be another global economic crisis?
- What is the most significant issue, other than Brexit, facing UK business interests?
- I've got no questions, but you have got five minutes to convince me you should have a place to study here.
- How will the relaxation of the tethering of the Chinese yuan to the US dollar affect this country's economy?
- What is the difference between a U-shaped and a V-shaped recession?
- What is the difference between management and leadership?
- A new country is formed in Africa. They introduce a new currency. How does the international market value what it is worth?
- Can we really measure GDP?
- What do you think you could contribute to college life?

- Talk about a recent article or book you read that you found interesting and tell us why.
- What do you expect to get out of this degree?
- Why is the course suitable for you?
- I see you have read X recently. Can you summarise the main arguments?
- Tell me about a difficult situation in the past five years that you dealt with badly and explain how you could have handled it better.
- What achievements in the last five years are you most proud of?
- What are your strengths? Give some examples.
- What are your weaknesses? How do you plan to overcome them?

Current issues

Should you be called for interview, the interviewer will probably be looking for a proven interest in and knowledge of current economics issues and/or business case studies. You should already be watching the news and reading relevant publications and newspapers, but you will need to do some extra preparation before you attend an interview. This section is designed to give you an idea of the types of issues that may come up at interview. You will need to do some additional preparation yourself to make sure you are up to date with what has been happening since this guide was published.

The turbulence in the global financial markets after 2008 and the unprecedented impact of Covid-19 demonstrate the unpredictability of the world of business and finance. Most people would not have guessed that some mortgage companies in the United States that lent money to people with very low incomes would have been the trigger for the collapse of banks and plummeting share prices across the world. Nor would many people have guessed that some EU countries that had experienced significant growth could now be described in the newspapers as being 'bankrupt'. Almost no one was expecting a global pandemic and the subsequent need for extended periods of lockdown and social distancing, which has had a significant and negative impact on economic activity. Further, fluctuating oil prices, arising from a range of factors including political unrest and terrorism, have had an enormous impact on people's lives. Things move very fast in the financial and business worlds: demands change, companies grow and collapse, and political issues affect prices and markets.

By the time you read this, many of the issues that made the headlines at the time of writing will no longer be relevant, and there will be new topics that I could not have predicted making the front pages. Above all, your knowledge of business, economics and management issues needs to be current. In this chapter, I have included a brief summary of some of the areas that you need to be familiar with. But beware: this is not a comprehensive list, and some of the topics may not be relevant by the time you are applying for your university courses. You must ensure that you prepare properly for your application by reading the quality newspapers on a daily basis, using websites such as www.bbc.co.uk/news to find out what is happening in your particular field of interest, reading magazines such as *The Economist* and watching the news on television.

The credit crunch, global financial crisis and economic recovery

The global financial crisis of 2007–2008 started with problems in the US housing market. A rise in interest rates caused many people to default on their mortgages, because the mortgage companies had lent them more money than they could afford to pay back. The term 'sub-prime mortgages' describes home loans given to people with very low incomes. The mortgage companies often sold the debts to banks, and so the problem began to escalate. We then began to read about the 'credit crunch' – a shortage of money available for banks to lend to other banks or the public. Some banks collapsed because they ran out of money. When banks collapse, the markets and the public lose confidence because savings are at risk and this has a knock-on effect on share prices.

Most countries were emerging from the recession by late 2009/early 2010.

Covid-19 and the economic impact

Covid-19 is an infectious disease caused by a newly discovered coronavirus that seems to have begun to infect human beings towards the end of 2019 in the Hubei province of China before spreading world-wide in 2020. At the time of writing (late January 2023), there have been over 667 million confirmed cases and almost 6.7 million deaths. Governments have responded in a number of ways to minimise the rate of infection in their respective countries – social distancing, country-wide and regional lockdowns, and enforced mask wearing are a few of the most common policies.

As one would expect, the pandemic has had a massive negative impact on the economy, both in the UK and globally. In April 2020, UK GDP fell 20%. This is the largest monthly drop in GDP since records began, and ten times larger than any single drop recorded before the emergence of Covid-19. Applying economic theory, GDP is the sum of an economy's levels of consumption (spending by consumers), investment, government spending and net trade (exports minus imports). Clearly, consumers spent far less in 2020/21 than average – enforced closures of shops and businesses, restrictions on people's movements, social distancing and limited capacity to spend time with individuals outside immediate family, as well as reduced confidence, are all contributing factors. Investment has also taken a considerable hit – there is little incentive for individuals and companies to invest in businesses during a period of economic recession and huge uncertainty. In terms of trade, the Office for National Statistics (ONS) reports that trade fell in both exports and imports by £33.1 billion (19.3%) and £29.9 billion (17.6%) respectively. The only component of GDP that has risen is government spending (the government has so far spent almost £300 billion on measures to fight Covid-19 and keep businesses afloat), although this is significantly outweighed by negative consumption, investment and trade.

Although the economic outlook feels very bleak, it is important to remember the economy is in recession for very different reasons to the recession of 2007–08 (see page 69). It took almost a decade for problems to build up as they did in the US sub-prime housing sector, and there existed fundamental and endemic problems within our global financial system. The economic fallout of Covid-19 is, in many ways, the result of putting large chunks of the economy on hold, in suspended animation, with the aim of minimising infections and deaths due to the virus. Despite the greatest-ever decline in GDP in the second quarter of 2020, the economy rebounded at record rates in the third quarter – reflecting the re-opening up of the economy and temporarily stifled demand. So, perhaps, we are not in as much trouble as the headlines make out – certainly the speed at which vaccines and treatments evolve are important determining factors.

Looking ahead, there is the rising risk of the UK entering recession, along with other major economies in Europe. As the then Chancellor of the Exchequer, Rishi Sunak, stated in his speech in November 2020, the 'economic emergency' caused by Covid-19 may have only just begun.

Inflation, which has risen through 2021, was partly a result of the disruption to global supply chains and a surge in energy prices. UK unemployment fell to a rate of 3.7% in January–March 2022, which was the lowest unemployment rate since 1974. Youth employment saw a quick recovery from spring 2021, returning to almost pre-pandemic levels by January–March 2022.

Oil prices

The global supply of oil is controlled by a cartel of oil-producing countries, the Organization of Petroleum Exporting Countries (OPEC), which pumps nearly half of the world's oil and decides how many barrels of oil can be sold each month, to ensure that its members get the best possible rewards from their resources. The global price of oil is governed by supply and demand, and by market feelings about the political situation in the OPEC countries (which may increase or restrict supply) and the economic situation in consumer countries (which may increase or reduce demand). Over the last few years oil prices have fluctuated dramatically.

Technological advances have meant the US has more than doubled its oil production in the last decade, impacting well on the American economy but causing concerns for OPEC producers. In 2014 the oil price dropped 28% from June to November, to its lowest level in four years. OPEC countries were keeping pumps on despite a glut in the market, amid concerns that this was an attempt to shut down competition from the US shale oil industry. Saudi Arabia's then oil minister, Ali Naimi, told Reuters that 'Saudi oil policy has been constant for the last few decades and it has not changed today'. He added that 'We do not seek to politicise oil ... for us, it's a question of supply and demand, it's purely business.' However, one political impact of the falling oil prices has been the damage to the finances of the Russian Federation, and the NATO powers are keen to reduce their reliance upon Russian natural gas.

At the beginning of 2016 oil prices fell below $30, but there was a modest recovery during the year, slightly undermined by the election of Donald Trump in early November 2016. Oil prices reached their last peak in October 2018 (at over $80), but then suffered their worst monthly drop since July 2016. Equities also saw a big sell-off during this month, suggesting the drop in oil prices was tied to broader concerns about the state of the economy. More recently, oil prices have plummeted during 2020 due to the economic fallout of Covid-19 and the collapse in demand for oil caused by global lockdowns. OPEC have responded by reducing production significantly, and this allowed prices to stabilise in the third quarter of 2020.

A fall in the price of oil is particularly damaging to oil-exporting economies (i.e. Russia and Saudi Arabia), who rely on tax revenue from the production of oil to fund government-spending programmes and infrastructure projects. For example, oil revenues in Saudi Arabia fell over 20% in the first quarter of 2020. When the price of oil rises, it affects airlines, businesses, households and the cost of goods. If consumers are spending proportionately more on oil-derived products, their spending on other goods and services will reduce. Because oil is used for transportation in all industries, the overheads of business will increase. This may either be passed on to the consumer, or, if this isn't possible, companies may have to reduce spending in other ways such as by making staff redundancies. For net importers of oil, price hikes may mean devoting more attention to exports to maintain a healthy balance of trade. In 2022, petrol and diesel prices reached record highs as the cost of living crisis continues.

Environmental issues

Fluctuating oil prices, diminishing stocks of fossil fuels and, above all, global warming have changed the ways in which businesses and governments operate. There is a growing awareness among consumers and politicians that changes have to be made, and that 'going green' is going to be more than just an altruistic aim. More and more businesses are now trying to market themselves as being friendlier to the environment than their competitors, and governments are keen to show potential voters that they are doing the same.

The Paris Climate Agreement is an environmental accord adopted in 2015 that aims to address climate change and limit global warming. Both the United States and China (who together represent about 40% of global emissions) signed up to the agreement, along with 174 states and the European Union. The specific objective of the agreement is to keep a 'global temperature rise this century well below 2 degrees Celsius above pre-industrial levels and to pursue efforts to limit the temperature increase even further to 1.5 degrees Celsius'.

However, in 2019, the Trump administration officially withdrew the US from the Paris Climate Agreement, citing the 'draconian financial and economic burdens the agreement imposes on our country' as the reason for the withdrawal. Following the November 2020 US presidential election, Joe Biden pledged to re-join the accord, and experts have commented that Biden's policies could reduce global heating by 0.1 degrees Celsius, bringing the goals of the Paris agreement back within reach. Further, Xi Jinping (China's president) has pledged to reach net-zero emissions by 2060. Some commentators feel some healthy competition between these two economic powerhouses would be a very good thing for the environment.

The global outbreak of Covid-19 had an impact on the environment due to the large-scale reduction in economic activity. Cleaner air, less water pollution and newly audible birdsong were all positive externalities of this pandemic. China can be used as an example here: manufacturers desperate to make up for lost time have pushed pollution levels back to pre-Covid levels already, according to a study by the *National Geographic*.

You should also be aware of the traded pollution permit scheme operating in the EU, the Emissions Trading Scheme (ETS). It is the largest greenhouse gas emissions trading scheme in the world. An emissions trading scheme, or a 'cap-and-trade' scheme, is a policy designed to incentivise companies to invest in 'green' or low-carbon technologies. The scheme allows businesses to buy permits, or carbon allowances, via an auction system. The permits are tradable so that if a business emits less carbon than their permit allows, it can sell the remainder of their carbon allowance to another business which is going to breach their quota. Over time, the supply of permits is gradually reduced, increasing the price of permits and incentivising businesses to invest in low-carbon technologies, rather than continuing to purchase allowances at higher prices.

Immigration

The impact of immigration is also widely debated. Some political groups argue that migrant workers drive down wages and take money from a benefits system they have contributed little towards. *The Economist* published an article which focused on the findings of Christian Dustmann of UCL and Tommasso Frattini of the University of Milan. Both scholars reported that between 1995 and 2011 migrant workers made a net positive contribution of more than £4 billion to the UK economy. They looked at the share of the cost of immigrants and the amount of revenue these workers contributed to the economy. Looking at the more controversial arrivals from Eastern Europe shows this group consistently make a positive net contribution. The findings indicated that these immigrants are less likely to claim benefits and live in social housing. Despite the academic discussion of the relative benefits for immigration, the public perception of the negative consequences of mass migration was a major factor in the victory for the proponents of Leave during the June 2016 EU referendum. Analysis of Home Office data shows that there has been an increase in non-EU visas, particularly from Ukraine and Hong Kong. However, EU migration has fallen, causing a gap to be filled by non-EU migrants. This will cause an increase in wage costs for firms, which would drive up prices.

Globalisation

When the UK joined the EU it was known as the Common Market because it broke down barriers for trade between the member countries and imposed some uniformity on trading conditions. Globalisation means that the marketplace has opened up to such an extent that it is very easy to include the entire world. Communication, transport, raising of finance and so on have all become much easier and firms have adapted their business strategies accordingly to improve the way they organise their business. Over half of all international trade is from one part of a multinational to another in a different country.

The standard wage in China has historically been low and firms obviously find it worth their while to build state-of-the-art factories there and ship the goods to their markets in Europe or the US, although the Chinese government's introduction of new labour laws in 2008 saw some multinational companies shift production to neighbouring countries such as Vietnam. Minimum wages are reviewed annually by Chinese provinces, and are continually on the rise – in 2018, half of

China's mainland regions increased their minimum wages. These rises are designed to increase domestic consumerism and may result in more companies moving from China to regions where labour is cheaper.

At first, it was only manufacturing jobs that transferred to the Far East to take advantage of low labour costs; however, more recently, India in particular has become a nucleus for service-industry jobs such as call centres and computer programming. It is obviously impossible for the West to compete against these wage levels and so it has to make the most of those aspects of business where it still has a competitive advantage – in particular, new business ideas.

Businesses in Europe and the US are developing better and ever more efficient ways of managing their brands. 'Think global, act local' is a slogan that is often used in this context to mean that, despite globalisation, different cultures are still more different than we might think. Unless you have a truly international brand such as McDonald's or Coca-Cola, your product might need to be slightly modified for each country.

The West also still has an advantage in technology and innovation, but it is not always easy persuading people to continue paying for this intellectual property. The fact that we can download a lot of open-source software from the internet means that many people no longer pay the licence fee to Microsoft, while MP3s enable people to listen to music without paying royalties to the musicians.

The alleged consequences of globalisation played a significant role in the success of Donald Trump in securing the Republican nomination for the US presidential race and eventually winning the election in November 2016. He campaigned strongly against open borders and trade agreements. This was also a factor in the UK's June 2016 referendum, during which many voters rejected the European Union as a distant and unresponsive institution which was ignoring the wishes of ordinary people.

In February 2022, Russia declared war on Ukraine, and the war was still ongoing at the time of writing in January 2023. Due to the war (and the after-effects of Covid-19), protectionist policies, even on a temporary basis, are increasing. This is reducing the competitiveness of countries, reducing GDP, and negatively affecting living standards.

The impact of terrorism

The international threat of terrorism is having an impact on the global economy, but some sectors are feeling the impact more than others. Travel and tour companies have taken the biggest battering to date, due, in the short term, to the psychological impact on consumers who are afraid to fly or visit tourist locations in some parts of the world. Supermarkets, on the other hand, are still trading comfortably, as people are feeling safer closer to home and are not neglecting their regular routines in the light of heightened terror alerts. In 2022, the number of terrorist attacks increased by 17%.

Terrorism can have both a direct and an indirect bearing on the economy. It directly affects the economy in the short term with the damage done to people's lives and property, the immediate responses to the emergency and rebuilding of the damaged systems, buildings and infrastructure. These costs, however, tend to be proportional to the scale of the attack sustained. The indirect costs of terrorism mean that investors and consumers lose their confidence in the economy. Strong consumer confidence often goes a long way towards boosting an economy, a particular example being in the US prior to the 2001 terror attacks, and the economy suffers as this confidence wanes. The threat of terrorism can also potentially affect productivity negatively, in the sense that transaction costs may be increased by higher insurance premiums and counter-terrorism regulations. The impact that terrorism has on the global economy is being continually assessed, and its full impact will depend on how long the campaign against terrorism continues and how quickly consumer confidence can be regained.

Brexit and the EU

Alongside the economic fallout of the Covid-19 pandemic, a dominant issue in both business and economics will be the implications for the UK economy of the Brexit vote of June 2016. Britain formally cut ties with Europe at the end of the transition period on 31 December 2020. Recent data shows the impact of Brexit on the UK economy has overall been negative. Brexit has reduced trade in goods by 15% and GDP has fallen. The impact of Brexit is likely to be worse than the impact of the pandemic. At the end of 2021, UK GDP was 5.2% smaller than predicted models.

The impact of Brexit on the UK economy will rest heavily on the terms of any trade deal. The higher the costs of trading with the EU, the greater the negative impact on the UK economy.

Monetary policy and price stability

Monetary policy, the use of interest rates and quantitative easing (QE) to influence aggregate demand and achieve macroeconomic objectives, has been in the news since the start of the Covid-19 pandemic. In the UK, the Monetary Policy Committee (MPC) lowered interest rates in 2020 to 0.1% as a response to Covid-19. However, as inflation increased to over 10% at the end of 2022, the Bank of England's interest base rate rose to 3.5%, with predictions of rates being even higher in 2023. Interest rates have been increased to combat the UK's rising inflation, for which the MPC has a target of 2% per year. At the time of writing, inflation in the UK had reached 11%, the highest rate since

1982, and is partly caused by reduced gas reserves from Russia (as a result of the war in Ukraine) and Brexit. This rise in inflation and higher interest rates has contributed to the so-called Cost of Living Crisis, which has squeezed household incomes, reduced living standards, and brought about the increased use of food banks in the UK by over 46%.

Fiscal policy and the UK economy

Fiscal policy has also been in the UK news recently. When Liz Truss succeeded Boris Johnson as Prime Minister, she selected Kwasi Kwarteng as the new Chancellor of the Exchequer. However, both lost their jobs less than 45 days after selection due to their 'mini budget', which caused shockwaves across the national and global economy, and almost collapsed the UK pensions systems. Truss and Kwarteng, both keen to pursue a more free-market approach to fiscal policy, planned to slash taxation and cut government spending. However, international confidence in the UK fell almost instantly as the tax cuts would worsen the fiscal deficit and national debt of the UK, which increased to its highest levels since the pandemic.

As a result, the value of the pound collapsed, causing a bailout by the Bank of England and a surge in government spending. This also caused an increase in mortgage repayments, and the value of pensions has subsequently fallen. While Liz Truss has been replaced by Rishi Sunak, the problem of an increasing fiscal deficit and national debt remains.

Make sure you read the news (ideally a business newspaper such as the *Financial Times*) regularly to keep up with economic implications as they unfold.

Entrepreneurs

Programmes such as BBC's *Dragons' Den* have raised the profile of the entrepreneur (defined by *The Oxford Dictionary* as 'a person who sets up a business or businesses, taking on financial risks in the hope of profit'). Well-known British entrepreneurs include James Dyson, inventor of the 'bagless' vacuum cleaner, Alan Sugar (Amstrad) and Richard Branson (Virgin).

Although *Dragons' Den* is a very successful entertainment programme, it has highlighted the opportunities and pitfalls of trying to start a small business and, in particular, the steps and capital needed to turn an idea into a profit-making venture. The contestants are quizzed on their marketing plans, the protection of their ideas through patenting, and on how the investors (the titular 'Dragons') would get a return on their investments.

Business case studies

An unexpected or unanticipated event can have a significant impact in the business world. If you are applying to study a business or management subject, you should have some examples at your fingertips of how (and why) companies and businesses grow, decline, change, adapt or develop. So it is vital to keep up to date with such events and the implications of each. Below is a list of case studies you could look at.

Possible case studies

Below are some suggestions for your research (a very small selection of the many fascinating areas of business that you could look at).

- Volkswagen emissions scandal: several million VW diesel engines had been fitted with a defeat device that was able to detect when the cars were being tested, changing the cars' performance and thus improving the results of the emissions tests.
- Attempted takeover of UK pharmaceutical company AstraZeneca by US competitor Pfizer, and shareholder pressure to accept bid.
- Tesco shares' slump following an accounting error which led to the company being investigated by the Serious Fraud Office.
- AT&T's attempt to purchase Time Warner.
- The vegan food industry.
- Netflix, TV streaming services and the optimisation of DVD rental.
- How the large sportswear companies have acted in the face of negative publicity about the use of Asian 'sweatshops' that produce their expensive clothes, shoes and sports equipment very cheaply.
- How the impact of increasingly successful streaming service Spotify has affected Apple's dominance of the music download market.
- The role of social media in shaping businesses (www.twitter.com lists a number of case histories of how Twitter has been used by companies such as MTV and Cadbury).
- The impact of Covid-19 on the high street and the urban economy.
- Snapchat's 'unicorn' IPO and the justification for such a high valuation given the business is not yet profitable.
- Machine learning and AI technology – consider digital health and education technology.
- Growth of the CBD (Cannabidiol) market in the US, Europe and UK.
- The revolution of Zoom virtual hosting in 2020.
- Upgrading businesses' safety and efficiency through cybersecurity, automation, remote work, and data analysis.

For further examples of business case histories, see the latest edition of *The Times 100 Business Case Studies* online at https://business casestudies.co.uk.

7 | Non-standard applications

Not all students who apply for degree courses are studying A levels or their equivalent. The term 'non-standard' could be applied to many different scenarios. Perhaps you are studying for a mixture of examination qualifications, or you have had a gap in your education. You might have already started a degree course in another discipline and want to change direction. Whatever your situation, the first thing you should do is make contact with some universities (either by telephone or via the email addresses given on the university websites) to explain your situation and ask for advice.

We will look at two of the more common types of non-standard application in more detail: mature students and international students applying from their own countries. These non-standard applicants make up a significant proportion of those wanting to get on to business, economics and management courses.

Mature students

You are considered a mature student if you are 21 years old or older at the start of your undergraduate course. Mature students make up nearly a third of the UK's student population.

Mature students fall into three categories:

1. those with appropriate qualifications – for example, A levels – but who did not go to university and are now applying after a gap of a few years
2. those applying for a second degree, having graduated in a different discipline
3. those who have no A levels or equivalent qualifications.

If you are in the first two of these categories, you can apply using the same route as first-time applicants. However, it is worth contacting universities directly to discuss your situation with them and obtain their advice.

If the third category applies to you, A levels or other equivalent qualifications need not be the only entry pathway. In particular, the Access to Higher Education (HE) Diploma is open to all students aged 19 and over, and is recognised by universities as an alternative to more traditional qualifications for entry to undergraduate courses. Access to HE Diplomas are taught at Further Education colleges in the United Kingdom. To apply for a place, you need to contact the course provider directly for details of the application process. The large majority of courses begin in September, with the application process kicking off in January, but start dates and application periods can vary. For more information, please go to the Access to HE Diploma website: www. accesstohe.ac.uk. Please note, Access to HE Diplomas aren't taught in Scotland, but there are similar courses available there through the Scottish Wider Access Programme (SWAP).

Mature students apply using the same application process as school-leavers (i.e. in categories 1 or 2, opposite), which is by registering on UCAS's online system, the UCAS Hub (www.ucas.com). Whereas a student who is at school or college (or who is taking a gap year) will answer 'yes' to the question 'Are you applying through a school or college?' (and will then be asked for a 'buzzword' – a password that identifies their school or college), mature students will submit the form independently. The main difference is that when the school/college student completes the form, it will be forwarded to the person writing the reference, who will in turn send it to UCAS, whereas the mature student will add the referee details to the form. The referee will then be contacted by UCAS with a login so that they can upload their reference. The choice of a suitable referee depends on the applicant's situation: it could be a current or recent employer, someone who once taught the applicant, or someone who knows the applicant well. If you are in this situation, make sure that your referee reads the information on the UCAS website about how to write a reference, to ensure that it contains the information that the selectors are looking for. The other main difference for mature students will be in the 'Employment' section of the UCAS form. This should be as detailed as possible, and any gaps – for instance, if you have been travelling – should be explained either in the personal statement or by the referee.

International students

According to UCAS, the demand from international applicants for higher education degrees has continued post-pandemic and increased from 2021 to 2022. In 2022, almost 150,000 international students applied, with the highest number of offer holders being from China (+13.4% on 2021), India (+43.7%) and Nigeria (+32.7%). Almost all institutions have a dedicated international team able to give advice on applications and accommodation and to support you while you are in the UK. It is well worth making contact with these teams at your chosen universities to find out how they can help you.

International students fall into three categories:

1. those who are following A level (or equivalent) programmes either in the UK or in their home countries
2. those who are studying for local qualifications that are recognised by the UK as being equivalent to A levels
3. those whose current academic programmes are not equivalent to A levels.

Students in the first category will apply through UCAS in the normal way. All of the information in this book is applicable to them.

Students studying for qualifications that are accepted in place of A levels can also apply through UCAS in the normal way, from their own countries. The UCAS website (www.ucas.com) contains information on the equivalence of non-UK qualifications. Among these are the Irish Leaving Certificate and the European Baccalaureate. Information on the equivalence of other qualifications can be found on the UK government's qualifications website (www.enic.org.uk).

The UCAS website has a section for international students that explains the application process clearly. If you are not familiar with making UCAS applications, I would strongly recommend you visit the UCAS site and familiarise yourself with the process as soon as you can, as it can seem complicated. You can contact the UCAS customer service centre or your university choices if you require further help or advice.

The vast majority of international students will require a new visa to study for a degree course. From 5 October 2020, students from outside the UK who need a visa to study at UK universities and colleges will apply for a student visa – you can apply online through the gov.uk website. This new student route is the same for all international students, including those coming from the EU, EEA and Switzerland, and replaces the previously used Tier 4 visa system.

Universities will also want reassurance you have the sufficient language skills to cope with the course, and will ask international students to take a language test. Different universities require different tests and different minimum grades; IELTS, TOEFL, PTE Academic and Cambridge English Advanced are the most common tests.

Students who do not have UK-recognised qualifications will need to follow a pre-university course before applying for the degree course. These include:

- Foundation courses at UK colleges and universities – these normally last one year (for example, see www.ncuk.ac.uk)
- Foundation courses set up by, or approved by, UK universities or colleges, but taught in the students' home countries
- A level courses (normally two years, but in some cases this can be condensed into one year) in schools and colleges in the UK.

A levels or equivalent qualifications, such as the IB, allow students to apply to any of the UK universities, including the top-ranked universities such as Oxford, Cambridge and the LSE; however, Foundation courses are now recognised by many UK universities. You should check with your preferred universities about which courses they accept before committing yourself. Representatives of UK universities, schools and colleges regularly visit many countries around the world to promote their institutions and to give advice. You can also contact the British Council to get help with your application (www.britishcouncil.org).

If you are from an EU country, you are no longer eligible for home fee status, as a result of the UK leaving the EU. Each university sets its own fees for EU students, so it is important you check with the universities you are applying to for information about fees. There are some nuances and exceptions to this rule (e.g. if you are an Irish national, these changes do not apply), so it is important you do your own research. See www.gov.uk/guidance/studying-in-the-uk-guidance-for-eu-students   for the latest guidance for EU students applying to study in the UK.

In 2021, UCAS launched Myriad, a single postgraduate gateway aimed at international postgraduate students coming to the UK. It provides various support and guidance, such as on courses, accommodation, scholarships, funding and local jobs. Check the Myriad website for more details (www.myriad.ucas.com). Over 90% of UK universities and colleges are listed on Myriad, supporting students in 150 countries across the globe.

UK students applying to study abroad

If you want to spend part of your time at university abroad, you could look at either choosing a course that incorporates a year abroad (usually a four-year course in total), or spending part of your time overseas through the new Turing Scheme, which replaced Erasmus+ in the wake of Britain leaving the European Union.

The Turing Scheme is a UK government programme that contributes to their commitment to a Global Britain. This competitive grant funding scheme helps successful organisations from the UK and British Overseas Territories to fund individuals undertaking education and training in the UK and across the world. Funding helps participants cover travel expenses and costs of living, and helps with administrative funding for delivering the projects. The scheme helps organisations enhance their existing international ties and form new relationships around the world. During the 2022/23 academic year, the Turing Scheme supported nearly 40,000 students, including around 20,000 from disadvantaged backgrounds, to study and work around the world. For more details on the Turing Scheme, see www.turing-scheme.org.uk.

If you decide you want to study abroad for the whole of your course, there are some things to consider.

When starting your research, you will need to check that the institutions you are considering are reputable and that the qualification you'll be awarded is likely to be recognised in other countries. You can check this on the UK ENIC website (www.enic.org.uk). Recognition of your degree is even more important if you plan to work in a field where a qualification is an essential requirement (such as law, accounting or medicine). If you're unsure, you can check with the appropriate professional body in the country where you plan to work after you graduate.

There are lots of options for studying overseas in the English language – you don't necessarily have to study in an English-speaking country as it is increasingly common across Europe for courses to be offered in English. Also, you can apply to overseas universities as well as for UK universities at the same time. Once you have your results you are free to choose whether to remain in the UK or study abroad. However, please keep in mind that any students wishing to study their whole degree course in the EU may be subject to different fee rates in the future as a consequence of Brexit.

If you plan to travel further afield, you will need to research visa requirements and other practicalities, such as whether this will allow you to work while you study and whether you can apply for any funding, before making a decision. See the UK Council for International Student Affairs website (www.ukcisa.org.uk) for further information and advice on where to start.

Most countries do not have a central admissions service like UCAS, so it is likely you will need to apply to each course or institution individually.

Students with disabilities and special educational needs

Every year, over 60,000 applicants with physical disabilities, mental health conditions and/or learning difficulties apply through UCAS. If you have a disability or special educational needs, it is a good idea to contact the universities you are considering before you make your final choices. Speak to their student support departments and find out how the institution will be able to support you – this might come in the form of extra funding, a note-taker, specialist equipment, etc., and may be an important factor to consider when making your final choices.

An institution cannot discriminate against you based on your disability, so contacting it will not disadvantage your application (under the Equality Act 2010 it is unlawful to treat applications from disabled students less favourably). Institutions have a legal obligation to make 'reasonable adjustments' so that you are not substantially disadvantaged by your condition and are required to do everything they can to foster an environment where all students are treated equally by staff and other students.

The UCAS website has some good information for disabled applicants and recommends asking the following questions (to be tailored depending on the nature of your disability).

- Are all the buildings I need to use physically accessible?
- Are there any particular facilities for disabled students?
- Are there any current students with a similar impairment?
- What support do they receive?
- Who will help organise my support?
- Can you help me apply for additional funding if needed?
- Are the teaching and assessment methods appropriate to my needs?
- What would happen if I started the course and experienced a problem?

If you are planning to stay in university accommodation and your disability might be important in deciding where you live, make sure you speak to the accommodation or student services department as soon as you can. This will help it to prepare in advance and consider issues such as access arrangements, distance from your faculty buildings and any other special requirements.

Additional funding

Ask your chosen universities about additional funding and do some research into the Disabled Students' Allowance (DSA) as you may be eligible for this. You can receive DSA if you can provide evidence that your condition affects your ability to study. DSAs are there to financially support disabled students, where a cost is incurred as a direct result of your disability or specific learning difficulty. The amount you qualify for does not depend on your household income, and it does not have to be paid back. Depending on your needs, extra support from the DSA could include specialist equipment, travel costs, Braille paper, a note-taker or a photocopying allowance. (See also www.accessforstudents.com.)

UCAS also provides advice, including information on the financial support available to students with disabilities who are applying to university degrees as well as apprenticeships; see www.ucas.com/undergraduate/applying-university/individual-needs/disabled-students.

Also, make sure you let your funding body know as soon as possible if you think you might need extra help or equipment on your course. The UK funding bodies are:

- Student Finance England: www.gov.uk/student-finance-register-login
- Student Finance Wales: www.studentfinancewales.co.uk
- Student Awards Agency for Scotland (SAAS): www.saas.gov.uk
- Student Finance Northern Ireland: www.studentfinanceni.co.uk.

8 | Results day

The A level results will arrive at your school on the third Thursday in August. Scottish Higher results come out in early August, and International Baccalaureate results are issued in July. The universities will have received the A level and Scottish Higher results a few days earlier. You must make sure that you are at home on the day the results are published, or at least have access to a reliable internet connection. Do not expect universities to be sympathetic if you are calling from a youth hostel in Thailand. The date of results day is known at least 12 months before, so you have chosen to place yourself out of contact.

Don't wait for the school to post the results slip to you – get the staff to tell you the news as soon as possible. If you need to act to secure a place, you might have to do so quickly. This chapter will take you through the steps you should follow – for example, you might need to use the Clearing system because you have not achieved the grades that you needed. Results from other examination systems are not automatically sent to UCAS or to the universities, so you might need to email your results to the universities when you receive them.

A summary of the options available when you receive your results is discussed below.

If you have gained the grades that you need to satisfy your firm choice: congratulations, you have your place! The university will contact you with confirmation of the place. You'll need to have the following things ready to ensure that you can do everything you need to on results day:

- UCAS Hub login details
- UCAS ID number
- UCAS Clearing number, if you go into Clearing
- details of your offers
- the UCAS and Clearing numbers of your chosen universities
- a working phone and computer, so you can communicate by phone or email.

What to do if things go wrong during the exams

If something happens when you are preparing for or actually taking the exams that prevents you from doing your best, you must notify both the exam board and the universities that have made you offers. It's best if this notification comes from your headteacher, and it should include your UCAS personal ID number. Send it off at once: it is no good waiting for disappointing results and then telling everyone that you were ill at the time but said nothing to anyone. Exam boards can give you special consideration if the appropriate forms are sent to them by the school, along with supporting evidence.

Your extenuating circumstances must be convincing. A 'slight sore throat' won't do! If you really are sufficiently ill to be unable to prepare for the exams or to perform effectively during them, you must consult your GP and obtain a letter describing your condition.

The other main cause of underperformance is distressing events at home. For example, if a member of your immediate family is very seriously ill, you should explain this to your headteacher and ask him or her to write to the exam boards and universities.

What to do if you have no offer: UCAS Extra

If you apply for five courses and either receive no offers or decline all the offers you get, you are eligible for UCAS Extra. Extra operates from the end of February to the beginning of July and allows you to add one additional choice at a time. To find a course using Extra, use the UCAS search tool and the filter 'Show courses with vacancies'. Next, contact the universities and colleges listed to check if they'll consider you. To apply for the new course you need to add the details to your application. Your chosen university will consider your application and, if this is unsuccessful, you can add another Extra choice as long as it's before July. It's recommended that you call the university to which you want to apply before you add the Extra choice, to check whether there is space on the course and to discuss your suitability. If you have not heard back from the university within 21 days, you can add another Extra choice (again, before July).

Students who are not holding any offers when the examination results are published, or who have not been accepted by their choices because they have failed to achieve the grades that they need, are eligible for Clearing (see page 86).

What to do if you have an offer but miss the grades

If your grades are not close to those required for your firm choice but satisfy your insurance offer, you are automatically accepted on the insurance place. Check on UCAS Hub to see whether the insurance offer has been confirmed. If there seems to be a delay, contact the university.

If your grades are below those needed for your insurance offer, you are now eligible for Clearing (see below).

If your grades satisfy one of your offers, but you have changed your mind about the course you want to study, you can be considered for Clearing courses if you withdraw from your firm/insurance places. Contact UCAS to withdraw from your original place – you should be careful when doing this as you could end up with nothing if you are unable to find a Clearing place. A sensible option would be to contact your desired university to ask whether they would consider accepting you through Clearing before you withdraw from the course you are holding an offer for.

> If you have missing results (for example, an 'X' on your results slip rather than a grade), this probably means that there is an administrative error somewhere, for example a missing coursework mark, or no 'cash-in' code for your exams. Contact your school or college examinations officer immediately to sort out the problem. Contact your firm and insurance choices and explain the situation to them and ask them to hold your place until the problem has been resolved.

Clearing

Clearing is a system that allows students who are not holding any offers to try to get a place on a course with remaining vacancies. You can use Clearing if:

- you didn't receive any offers (or none you wanted to accept)
- you didn't meet the conditions of your firm and insurance choices
- you're applying after 30 June
- you've paid the multiple choice application fee of £27
- you've declined your firm place using the 'decline my place' button in your application.

You will be sent instructions by UCAS on Clearing automatically. You can search for new university courses using the Clearing search tool, and if you find the course you are interested in, you will need to contact that university yourself. The online Clearing search tool on the UCAS website is the only official vacancy list and the most up-to-date. Have your Clearing number ready and be prepared to answer questions about why you want to study the course. You can add only one Clearing choice, so only do this if you have received a verbal offer. When you receive a Clearing offer that you want to accept, log in to UCAS and press the 'Add a Clearing choice' button. Clearing places at the top universities are scarce, so you will need to act very quickly.

Recently, UCAS has introduced Clearing Plus for candidates who were unsuccessful with their application or are applying for the first time by using Clearing. To use Clearing Plus, you will need to click on the 'My matches' button, which will show the top 50 matches or courses that UCAS has found for you based on the information you provided in your application. If you are interested in any matches, click on 'interested' in your Hub to let those universities know that you would like to be considered. If they then contact you and choose to offer you a place, you will need to add that course into your Clearing choice on UCAS to confirm your decision to accept the offer.

What to do if your grades are better than expected

If you exceed your predicted grades and hold a firm unconditional offer but no longer want it because you have found a more suitable option, you can release yourself into Clearing by using the 'Decline your place' button in your application. Think carefully though and make sure you first speak to your university or college and/or an adviser at your school. *Only use the 'Decline your place' button if you are fully confident that your current firm choice is no longer suitable.* If you want to remain at the same university, but have found a different course requiring higher grades, you must first speak to the university or college.

Bear in mind that there are unlikely to be places on the most competitive courses in Clearing, but it is still worth having a look if you are in this situation.

Retaking your A levels

If you did not get the grades you were hoping for, you may choose to retake your A levels in the subjects that dragged your scores down. If you intend to reapply to university it is worth noting that the grade requirements for retake candidates are often higher than for first-timers.

Independent sixth-form colleges provide specialist advice and teaching for students considering A level retakes. Interviews to discuss this are free and carry no obligation to enrol on a course, so it is worth taking the time to talk to their staff before you embark on A level retakes. Many further education colleges also offer (normally one-year) retake courses, and some schools will allow students to return to resit subjects either as external examination candidates or by repeating a year.

Reapplying

If you plan to reapply through UCAS because you didn't receive offers, decided to withdraw from your application because you had changed your mind about a course or university, or because you did not meet the required grades, you will need to do some research. Some universities will not accept reapplications from students who failed to make the cut the previous year, so before you waste a place on your UCAS form check with the university to which you would like to apply that it is willing to consider a second application. The same can be said if you are applying to different universities but are retaking some or all of your A levels or other qualifications.

If you want to reapply to the same university, contact the admissions department to ask whether it is likely to consider your application. You should think carefully about reapplying to a university that did not offer you a place in your first attempt. As a retake student they are unlikely to change their mind during your second attempt. However, you could reapply to universities which offered you a place, even if you did not make them your firm or insurance choice the first time around. Universities want the best students, and if they liked your profile in the spring of 2024, they may well still favour your application in the spring of 2025 when you reapply.

You do not need to change your personal statement if you are applying for the same or similar courses. You may wish to update and amend the statement, but there is no obligation to completely revise your personal statement. It is not being lazy if the statement varies only slightly from the previous year. The reasons why you wanted to study geography in November 2023 are unlikely to significantly change by November 2024. If you received none or few offers the previous year you may wish to revisit the statement, or if you have undertaken any relevant additional work experience, for example, it would be worth including this on the personal statement. However, if you reconstruct a personal statement that secured five offers the previous year, you perhaps risk damaging your future chances; instead spend your time more usefully elsewhere, for instance, researching courses and universities.

Also, as noted in Chapter 5, UCAS is reforming UK Admissions, and the personal statement is one of the areas that is very likely to undergo changes in the next UCAS cycle. Therefore students are strongly advised to check the UCAS website for the most recent updates (www.ucas.com/about-us/news-and-insights/reforming-admissions).

9 | Fees and funding

Studying is expensive. Unfortunately, the reality of being a student is that you are likely to have incurred considerable debt by the time you graduate. This chapter will guide you through how much your course is likely to cost and what funding is available to help you.

Tuition fees

The tuition fees you will have to pay for undergraduate courses will depend on where you live and where you intend to study (see below). You can find more information on www.gov.uk/repaying-your-student-loan.

For UK students, the fees do not have to be paid at the start of each year. You are effectively given a loan by the government that you repay through your income is over the following thresholds:

- £25,000 per annum for students from England
- £27,295 per annum for students living in Wales
- £20,195 per annum for students in Northern Ireland
- £25,375 per annum for Scottish students.

Students from England

Students from England studying in England, Northern Ireland or Scotland will pay fees of up to £9,250 per year, and up to £9,000 to study in Wales.

Students from Wales

Students from Wales pay up to £9,000 if they study in Wales, or up to £9,250 if they study in England, Scotland or Northern Ireland.

Students from Scotland

Students from Scotland studying at Scottish universities will not have to pay tuition fees. They still need to apply to SAAS to have their tuition fees paid, as this is not automatic. Scottish students will pay up to £9,250 if they study in England or Northern Ireland, and up to £9,000 if they study in Wales.

Students from Northern Ireland

Students living in Northern Ireland will pay up to £4,710 if they attend a university in Northern Ireland, up to £9,250 if they study in England or Scotland, and up to £9,000 if they study in Wales.

As stated on www.studentfinanceni.co.uk, Northern Ireland (NI) students include the following:

- UK or Irish citizens who have been living in the UK & Islands for three years before the first day of the first year of their course
- those who have been granted settled status and living in the UK & Islands for three years before the first day of the first year of their course
- those who have been granted settled status under the EU settlement scheme (or pre-settled status if you are an EU national) and been living in the UK & Islands for three years before the first day of the first year of your course.

International and EU students

There is no maximum amount universities are allowed to charge international students; the cost varies and can be found on the individual universities' websites.

As stated on www.gov.uk/student-finance/eu-students, you may be eligible for a Tuition Fee Loan and help with living costs if you're from an EU country, Iceland, Liechtenstein, Norway or Switzerland. However, to receive student finance you must have settled or pre-settled status under the EU Settlement Scheme. You should ask the relevant student funding body if you're eligible for any support if you're an EU student studying in Scotland, Wales or Northern Ireland.

Living costs

If you are planning to study full time, it is very unlikely that you will be able to work to support yourself. The amount you will need for rent, travel, bills, books, food and other living costs will depend largely on where you will be living. If you choose to live at home with your parents and go to a local university it will obviously be considerably cheaper than relocating to a major city and supporting yourself.

Maintenance loans

The government provides repayable loans to maintain students from England in education in addition to tuition fee loans. The figures for the 2023/24 academic year are:

Living at home	Up to £8,400
Living away from home, outside London	Up to £9,978
Living away from home, in London	Up to £13,022
Living a year of a UK course studying abroad	Up to £11,427

Figures and funding arrangements for students from different parts of the UK will vary slightly. For further details please refer to the UCAS website www.ucas.com and to the student funding website for your country.

England: Student Finance England www.gov.uk/student-finance

Wales: Student Finance Wales www.studentfinancewales.co.uk

Scotland: Student Awards Agency for Scotland www.saas.gov.uk

Northern Ireland: Student Finance NI www.studentfinanceni.co.uk

Additional funding

Some universities offer scholarships or bursaries. These may be offered on the basis of academic excellence, household income, sporting achievement or something else the university decides is relevant. An example of this is the UCL Faculty Undergraduate Scholarship for Excellence (£3,000 per year) offered by University College London, which is awarded for academic excellence. LSE also provides generous financial support, in the form of bursaries and scholarships to all students regardless of their fee status. It is a good idea to check directly with the student services department at your chosen university to see if you qualify for any such schemes. Bursaries do not need to be repaid and may come in the form of reduced tuition fees, cheaper accommodation or cash paid directly to you.

There are a number of publications that give details of funds and bursaries offered by educational trusts, including *The Guide to Educational Grants*, published by the Directory of Social Change. For scholarship information have a look at the scholarship search website (www.scholarship-search.org.uk).

Local Jobcentres also have details of sources of sponsorship from industry and some government departments.

Special considerations

Extra help is available for students with a disability, mental health condition or specific learning difficulty, and for students with children or adult dependants. Students from Wales and Northern Ireland may be entitled to receive a Special Support Grant (up to £3,475), while students from all parts of the UK are also eligible for additional support from their university. This may take the form of note-takers and scribes for dyslexic students, funds for specialist equipment or additional tutoring. See the appropriate support website for further information on support grants and contact the student support department of your university to see what support it will provide.

Sponsorship

Some employers offer sponsorship to students on a vocational degree course such as business or management studies. For example, Deloitte runs a Scholars Scheme that includes work placements before starting university and an annual bursary of £2,250 for three years of undergraduate study to a limited number of students from selected UK universities. Also, Airbus sponsors a Business degree apprenticeship, which integrates university study into on-the-job training. Barclays sponsors a Management & Leadership degree at Anglia Ruskin while KPMG, Experian, Morrisons, Nestlé, Co-op, Ernst and Young (EY) also support various courses.

It is also worthwhile enquiring about the availability of any sponsorships by writing directly to companies' personnel departments. You can also get in touch with the university department and the careers service as they may have contacts with particular employers favourably disposed towards sponsoring students. If you are successful, the deal is usually that you will work for the sponsoring organisation during the holidays. This can give you excellent experience and, if you perform well, the prospect of a job offer after you graduate. If you are seeking sponsorship, contact employers as early as possible, as it is common that applications need to be in well before the UCAS deadline.

International students

Fees for international students vary from university to university and from course to course. International students pay higher fees than home students. Whereas UK students will pay up to £9,250 a year, students from outside the UK can pay anything from £11,400 to £38,000. For example, annual tuition fees for BSc Economics for international applicants starting in 2023 is £26,592 at LSE, £27,500 at Manchester University and £29,830 at Warwick University.

You should contact your own country's education department, and look at UK universities' websites, for further information. Accommodation and meals will be extra. The cost of living depends on where you study, but, as a rough guide, about £930 a month should cover food, accommodation, books and some entertainment costs. Some governments will sponsor students for their studies in the UK, and some UK universities offer scholarships to students from particular countries, so you should check individual institutions' websites or contact the British Council in your country for more information.

10 | Career paths

Recent findings from the National Foundation for Employment Research (NFER) show that almost all of the new jobs created by 2035 will be in 'professional' and 'associate professional' roles. The Institute of Student Employers (ISE) reported that graduate salaries in 2022 rose the sharpest in 20 years, with some employers increasing salaries by 20%. Also, pay rates for apprentices are continuing to grow faster as employers compete in a tight labour market.

Graduates are also likely to earn more compared to non-graduates. The government's graduate labour market statistics found that between 2020 and 2021, the median salary for university leavers increased to £36,000. And in 2021, the median salary for graduates remained at £10,000 more than that of non-graduates.

Employment prospects vary depending on the degree you graduate with, and the good news is that business-related courses are among those that will lead to higher earnings. As can be found on www. explore/career-path, the median salary for economics graduates is now £48,000, compared to the median graduate salary of £32,000.

High Fliers Research conducted a study of the UK's 100 top employers and found that the number of graduate vacancies available now is 11% higher than the pre-pandemic peak recorded in 2019. Moreover, the latest recruitment targets for the country's top employers indicate the largest annual rise in graduate recruitment for more than 15 years. The number of graduate jobs on offer in 2022 was expected to increase by almost 16%.

Getting into business

Many graduates pursuing a business or financial career have degrees in the subject, but not all fall into this category. Some have studied another subject, such as statistics, psychology or English, and join a company on its graduate management-training programme. Others have completed vocational courses. It is also possible to become a successful businessperson by working your way up through the ranks from the shop floor – but this is much less common today than it was in the past.

Because managers and economists work in so many different businesses and organisations, and their roles vary from organisation to organisation, there is no single route to a career in these fields. However, you will need certain skills and talents, and a strong academic background helps.

Skills and qualities

A degree, even a very good one, is not enough to get on to a prestigious training scheme with a notable company. Graduate recruiters are not usually bothered about your particular degree subject – but they will often want their management trainees to be numerate. Subjects such as marketing, mathematics or statistics, economics, finance or business studies can give you an edge, but some employers still prefer the traditional academic subjects such as history or classics, even for marketing consumer products. However, there are no degree subjects that completely preclude a graduate from entry on to a management-training scheme.

Case study

'The competition to get on to the scheme was intense and we all really had to jump through hoops to secure our places. This started with a fairly straightforward one-to-one interview with the graduate recruitment manager on my university campus. I had prepared well for the interview and had done my research on the company, including looking at its website, and I think this really helped – it certainly gave me confidence. I'd also had a mock interview at my careers service, which was extremely useful. The next stage was an all-day event at the employer's premises. I was with about eight other candidates and we went through a combination of individual interviews with more senior staff and some group exercises, where they gave us a hypothetical problem and asked us to discuss it as a group and come up with some recommendations. I guess it didn't matter too much what our ideas were as long as they made some sense, but I think what they were really looking for was to see how we interacted with each other. That included how we communicated our ideas and also how we listened to others and took their ideas on board. We were also given a 30-minute numeracy test where we were not allowed to use a calculator – so remember to brush up on your tables! I must have passed all those tests, as I was then offered a place on the scheme to start the following September.'

Graham, Mathematics and Management graduate, now a graduate trainee

If you have a good academic background, it will be your personal qualities that will often win you the job. Most companies' recruitment brochures will give you a fairly comprehensive list of skills and qualities they are looking for. Here are some of them:

- communication skills (these are paramount)
- the ability to think logically and clearly and to analyse accurately
- the ability to research facts and to be able to assess what information is important
- absorption: assessment of the importance of lots of very detailed information and seeing its implications
- organisational ability
- the ability to work with anyone at any level and get the best out of them
- building and maintaining working relationships, and summing up people accurately
- the ability to co-operate and contribute to a team
- numeracy
- self-confidence
- sound business awareness
- natural authority and leadership
- the ability to think strategically, see the whole picture and conceptualise
- the ability to keep targets in focus and make sure they are reached
- the ability to motivate others, recognise their potential and delegate responsibility
- high ethical standards
- the ability to prioritise information and tasks.

Career opportunities

Business and management graduates

Graduates in business and management enter a very wide range of careers. These include accountancy, investment banking, insurance, management consultancy, information technology, marketing, business journalism, the media and the legal profession – to name but a few. The list of options is almost endless, but it must be highlighted that many of the careers, and the employers recruiting such graduates, are increasingly global.

How often do you hear someone say 'I'd like to work in business' or 'I'd like to be a manager'? These are not uncommon career aims, but more often than not people do not have a real understanding of what being a businessperson or manager actually involves. The terms are sometimes used as meaning 'being successful' rather than anything to do with the concept of the work. So, first things first: if you are thinking about a career in business or management, you need to find out what management means and what the typical functions or departments in businesses are.

Whenever you open a newspaper and look at the jobs section, every second advertisement has the word 'manager' in its title. Is this just a ploy to attract applicants or is it that some form of management is integral to many jobs? And if so, what do all these people do? Well, they all do different things, and work for an enormous variety of organisations. Yet at the same time they all have certain responsibilities and tasks in common.

The most straightforward definition of management in business terms could be 'the achievement of objectives through other people'. So, the primary difference between managerial and other types of work is that it involves getting other people to do the necessary work rather than doing all the tasks yourself.

Essentially, anyone who manages is responsible – and accountable – for making sure that whatever department or project they are in charge of runs smoothly and successfully. (Depending on the type of employer, this usually means profitably too!) Now this obviously means that you bask in the glory – and, with luck, the profits – when all goes well. But when things go wrong, as they inevitably do at times, the manager is the person who will be taken to task because it is he or she who is ultimately responsible for what happens. So you can draw the following conclusions about the role of management in business.

- Every job has some managerial aspects. Even the most junior clerical workers must ensure that others co-operate with them so that they can do their job.
- No job is exclusively managerial. Everyone has to perform some tasks for themselves.
- Management is not just about status or being paid better. Some professionals and other specialists with no real management responsibilities are often more senior and have a higher salary than many managers.
- The term management also covers a vast range of other activities, including supervision, organisation, administration and leadership. (The job title 'executive' is sometimes used in the same context as 'manager'.)

Management is undoubtedly a skill in its own right and is essentially the same in whatever field it is carried out. Good managers are not confined to managing work that they are capable of doing themselves. Indeed, in the higher levels of management, it can be an advantage not to have the bias that specialist knowledge can bring.

Economics graduates

Many economics graduates follow business or management careers. Economics degrees provide graduates with a range of analytical skills, and an in-depth knowledge of how domestic and global money markets operate. In particular, businesses that operate on a global scale are keen to recruit economists. There are many other opportunities open to economics graduates. Economists are employed by banks and other financial institutions, public bodies, political parties, governments, non-governmental organisations and universities. Newspapers often survey the UK's top companies or biggest employers, and the majority of these will employ economists. Some will be banks, accountancy firms or management consultants, but government bodies such as the NHS also recruit economists. The Government Economics Service (GES) employs over 3,500 economists, recruiting them throughout the year into civil service jobs. In addition to this, the GES runs five recruitment schemes, including a Degree Level Apprenticeship Programme. Good economists are able to analyse information, mostly in numerical form, and draw conclusions from it. They are generally strong mathematicians as well as being able to understand theoretical models and apply them to real-life situations.

Case study

Jenny studied A levels in Economics, Mathematics and Physics at a sixth-form college in London. She found all three subjects worked well together, and she was able to use ideas and techniques from her physics to help her with her economics.

'I found that being able to understand the ideas behind proving theories and equations in A level Physics was very helpful in my economics. In physics, you look at experimental results and then see how they can either prove, disprove or modify an equation or theory. A good example of this is in quantum physics, where one set of experiments seems to prove that light is a wave, whereas another set shows it is a particle – two very different things.

'Economics is the same, but the experiments are on a much larger scale – the global economy, for example! Economists come up with conflicting models to try to explain or predict how economies can develop and change, and we then try to see whether the results of the "experiment" – that is, what is actually happening in the world – support the theories.'

At university, Jenny chose an Economics degree course that involved a good deal of mathematical application, as she enjoyed this aspect of the subject. She now works for a large international bank, looking at the impact of changes in commodity prices and how they affect the economy.

Beginning your career

A number of large companies have graduate training schemes for new graduates. With such companies, training is usually undertaken in-house through formal programmes and on-the-job experience, and is sometimes combined with study for a professional qualification.

However, lots of graduates start their careers in small organisations that may not have any formal training programme. Although this is less structured, it is possible to get a wealth of early experience and responsibility by being thrown in at the deep end, while gaining an excellent overview of how the whole organisation operates.

There is no right or wrong answer when it comes to whether you join a big or small organisation initially. You should consider how much structure and formal training you want and look for an organisation that will give you this. If a firm belongs to the government initiative Investors in People, it will place great emphasis on training and career development. Traditionally, people reach a management position after a number of years of experience in a specialist function, such as sales, marketing, personnel or finance.

Many firms have moved away from the traditional hierarchical structure based on business functions (such as production, marketing, etc.) to one based on project teams. Working in a smaller team like this can be very exciting because there is often a greater sense of urgency and camaraderie among the various members. You need to learn how to reach decisions in a group and realise that everyone is different, but that this does not mean they do not have important skills to contribute. You also learn that no one is perfect and everyone can make mistakes – including you!

Information technology (IT) really has changed the way we are able to work. Some firms now even consist of 'virtual teams', i.e. people who work together but do not share an office. They may be scattered geographically and communicate via their mobile phones and the internet. They may even work for that company on only a few days every week, doing something else for the rest of their time.

One consideration is to delay the beginning of your career by studying for a master's degree, most notably a Master of Business Administration (MBA). There are many MBA courses in the UK. A useful website would be www.find-mba.com/most-popular/uk-ireland, which lists the 50 most popular courses in the UK and Ireland in terms of the number of views each receives. There are many different courses, so you need to establish a similar process to your undergraduate degree to find the right course for you.

There are relative advantages in pursuing a master's degree, but it is not a decision that needs to be taken in the final year of your undergraduate degree. Many graduates enter the job market, identify an area of interest and then search for an appropriate master's degree. Remember, if you enter the world of business and management, you are not limited to an MBA degree. You may wish to discuss your options with an employer, for many companies encourage their employees to further their education. You may be able to secure funding, time release and other forms of support. The key point is to keep your options open and undertake research before any further academic study.

Typical business functions

We will now look at some of the most popular areas of business and management in more detail.

Marketing

The marketing function in business is to make people aware that a product or service exists, and encourage people to buy it. This often requires identifying the most likely groups of buyers and targeting them in specific ways. TV advertising, for example, requires considerable planning and market research. Marketing professionals will have researched the product and its rivals and identified how and where they want to place their product in the market to maximise sales, promote brand loyalty or achieve market penetration, and so on. They will commission an advertising agency to come up with a suitable campaign and monitor how this affects sales. Psychologists are often involved in devising advertising slogans or images that will stick in the mind and that will be recalled or influence us when we see the product.

Careers in marketing are often varied; many people who have worked in marketing later move on to advertising agencies or to work as publicity consultants. Marketing tends to attract people who are creative and good at thinking up original and innovative ideas. However, there are also many jobs in market research that require people who can direct discussion groups, design and conduct surveys and process the statistical evidence. For these jobs, it is important to have good numeracy and communication skills.

Most business studies degrees will include modules on marketing. If you are sure that you want a career in marketing, you could decide to choose a joint honours degree such as business studies with marketing, or a single honours degree in marketing. Some art colleges will also offer specialised marketing degree courses, such as fashion marketing. These tend to involve more creative and practical work than those offered on the more traditional courses.

Case study

After graduating with a BA in Business Administration, Joanna decided she wanted to combine her qualification with her love of fashion. She became a marketing assistant at a global company and has worked her way up through the industry.

'The first job I had was a bit of a shock. Translating what I'd learnt in theory into practice was the biggest challenge and in hindsight this culture shock would have been limited if I'd had some more work experience. I got my head down and learnt as much as I could before deciding to work abroad. I worked as a marketing executive for a global retailer in Sydney. Whilst I enjoyed my role, I found that I was drawn to the more creative aspects of the industry. Upon my return to the UK I took an evening class in fashion journalism at the London College of Fashion and have since moved into fashion copywriting for a major online retailer of designer fashion. My background in business complements this more creative role and I think it enables me to see the bigger picture rather than just the objectives of my own role.'

Sales

Another aspect of business is sales. This work is increasingly paid on commission only. In other words, if you do not sell anything you do not get paid. On the other hand, if you are good at selling, the rewards can be fantastic.

What you sell will depend on the business you work in. Books, advertising, professional services, timeshares, cars, stocks and shares, ideas, computer software – anything that a business produces needs to be sold. The work may involve travelling as a rep or may be desk-based telesales, for example. As a manager you will also be responsible for the sales team, whether it is in-house or made up of reps based around the country or abroad.

You can be taught sales techniques as part of a business studies course, but you need a basic aptitude to sell really effectively. If you have natural selling skills, this might be an area to consider. If you are not sure whether a job in sales is for you, your summer holidays could be a useful testing period. There are lots of jobs where you could try out your sales technique, such as working on a stall in a fair or market and encouraging people to come and buy your products, or doing work experience in an estate agents or car showroom to see how the people working there use their sales techniques to encourage customers to make a purchase.

As well as being an integral part of a business-related degree, there are more specialised degree courses available that focus on this area, such as marketing and sales or sales management.

Case study

Neil has been working at a large retail outlet as a department manager for the past two years. He graduated three years ago with a 2.i degree in Business Studies from Kingston University and successfully got his job by applying through the university milk round. After taking a year off, which combined temporary work with travelling, he joined the company on its 18-month graduate training programme.

'My training has been excellent and I am still learning all the time. I have been on short courses covering topics such as teamwork, negotiating skills, customer service and management skills. I started my training in the soft furnishings department and am now the department manager for the books department. I have been exposed to all aspects of running a department, from working on the shop floor and serving customers to learning about stock-taking and display.

'Each day is totally different – you never know what to expect when dealing with customers. Most are very nice, but you do have to be tactful when dealing with tricky situations. You need plenty of stamina and flexibility, but the rewards are well worth the hard work when you see the sales figures boosted. And the satisfaction of working with your team is tremendous.'

Personnel

Personnel work, or human resources (HR) as it is often called, covers every aspect of a business relating to the people in it. As a personnel officer, you would be involved in the recruitment and training of staff, implementing company policies and government legislation affecting employees and maintaining employee records.

In large companies, HR departments analyse staffing requirements, agree targets and devise selection procedures. They organise staff appraisals and administer training and management development policies, and deal with disciplinary matters as they arise. Personnel departments in some very large organisations will often be split into different functions, such as training and graduate recruitment.

In smaller companies, there might be only one or two people who cover all personnel issues, and these may be a small part of their whole job function. So if you were to join a small administrative department you might get more of an overview of personnel than in quite a large company, where your training might be more specialised. In small companies, it is also quite common for departmental managers to deal with personnel issues such as training and discipline.

Personnel work is often challenging and emotionally demanding. The skills required include objectivity (the ability to see all sides of a problem), a reasonable level of numeracy, organising skills and an understanding of all types of people.

Management degrees are particularly suitable for students who are interested in following this route, because they will include modules on the psychology of dealing with people. There are also legal issues to be taken into consideration – these are also likely to be offered as part of a management-related degree. Most business courses will also provide students with the opportunity to find out more about personnel work and HR, but it is likely to form a smaller part of the course. You might also look at business and personnel or business and HR management courses.

Case study

Ryan graduated with a 2.i degree in Business Studies. He had done an industrial placement with a leading accountancy firm and was accepted on to its very competitive graduate training scheme. Ryan eventually plans to go into HR, but the firm he is working for requires all staff of a certain level to be qualified accountants, so he is currently going through his professional accountancy exams.

'It's tough and to be honest, accountancy does not appeal to me in the long run, but it will give me an understanding of the industry that would be impossible if I went straight into HR. Once I've completed my training, I'll be able to transfer to the HR department of my company and work abroad if I wish. I'll also always have my accountancy qualifications as a back-up.'

Finance

The financial aspects of a business are commonly regarded as the most important. If there is no cash in the tills and the bank wants the overdraft repaid yesterday, that spells trouble. All firms have accounts departments responsible for sending out invoices and chasing debtors, paying suppliers and drawing up the company's annual accounts. This is known as financial accounting and refers to keeping track of the financial side of the business after the transactions have happened. Financial accounting lets the senior management know how well the business has done in the past year. However, it does not prepare for the future.

Planning for the future is called management accounting. With this, firms draw up extensive and detailed budgets for every department so that they can keep a tight control on costs and are therefore less likely to make mistakes in the year ahead. Both types of accounting make extensive use of IT.

Accountancy does not have to be boring or deskbound. It can be a good way to join a creative team in the media industry or film industry – areas that are often difficult to get into otherwise.

The financial sector covers a wide range of careers and employers. These include banks, building societies, insurance companies and accountancy firms. All of these organisations would be open to recruiting graduates with a degree in business or management, as long as their A level grades (or equivalent) are good enough and they have a good degree, which usually means a minimum classification of 2.i.

All the major clearing banks run graduate training schemes that give you the opportunity to train and work in many aspects of the bank's function over a period of around 18 months. This will usually mean moving around the country for your various placements. You will normally be encouraged to study for the Chartered Banker Institute professional examinations. Once experienced, you might be promoted to, for example, a branch manager. In this role you could be involved with individuals and corporate clients. As a trainee, you might have a spell in a department marketing corporate services and then move into a role as a personal accounts executive.

In addition to their general graduate training schemes, most of the large banks also recruit graduates directly into their computing departments. This does not necessarily require you to have a computer science degree, and most of these training schemes are open to graduates from any discipline. Most careers in the financial sector will require you to be meticulously accurate and good with figures. You will also need to have good interpersonal skills, excellent IT skills and to be able to work effectively as part of a team.

Business studies, economics and management degrees will all cover aspects of finance and accounting, as these are equally applicable to the running of a small business, a government organisation or a country's economy. A business- or management-related degree will look at the more practical aspects of finance – accounting procedures, financial management, legal issues and banking procedures – whereas an economics degree will look at these issues on a larger scale and in a more mathematical and theoretical way.

There are also more specialised degrees available for those students who have a clear idea of their future direction: accounting, accounting and finance, and banking and finance courses are widely available and very popular.

Case study

Son started his BSc (Hons) Finance course in London at Bayes Business School (formerly known as Cass). In the first year, he participated in numerous events, including raising capitals for start-ups and the simulated IPO process. Unfortunately, during the end of his first year, the Covid-19 pandemic left Son with no choice but to go back home to Vietnam, where he studied online for two years.

'During my final year, I was introduced to the Vietnamese stock market. I used my finance knowledge that I learnt in university to conduct research into the market, in order to identify which companies were worth investing in. Throughout the year, I managed to keep pace with studying and raising funds from friends and family to start investing. The fact that I got exposed to the stock market facilitated my study. In the end, I managed to achieve a First Class Honours.

'Having graduated from university last summer, I got an internship at a stock brokerage firm, SSI Securities Corporation, due to my previous experience in investing in the stock market. After two months of training, I gained in-depth knowledge relating to how financial markets react to certain economic policies, how experts use financial models to evaluate companies' intrinsic value, and how to interpret financial ratios on the company's balance sheet. The valuable experience has helped me secure my new job with one of the leading investment firms in Vietnam, BIM Group.'

Purchasing

Most organisations, including manufacturing and insurance companies, as well as public-sector organisations, require expert purchasers or buyers.

'Purchasing' is a term mainly used in industry. 'Buying' tends to be used in retailing, and other organisations will often use the term 'supplies'.

But the principles of the job are the same. Purchasing managers are now part of a wider profession known as supply chain management. Purchasing is probably at its most complicated in the manufacturing industry, where products such as cars are assembled from many different components. The purchasing manager may be involved from the start, when the design engineers begin to specify the raw materials and the parts needed, by pinpointing suppliers and sorting out any problems with new designs.

Skills required for purchasing include the ability to work well with figures, accuracy, and the ability to digest technical and other data quickly and easily, as well as excellent communication skills.

Business and management degrees will cover topics that are relevant to students interested in this area, and are likely to use case histories and current businesses as illustrations. Economics degrees will include courses in microeconomics (which deals with how individuals and businesses manage and plan their finances) and macroeconomics (how countries' economies depend on income and expenditure). These courses will treat purchasing in a more theoretical and mathematical way. You could also investigate purchasing and supply, or business and purchasing degree courses.

Start-ups

The term 'start-up' first emerged in the 1970s, but only became popular at the beginning of the 21st century with small companies, usually in the field of technology and digital operations, offering an innovative or niche product with the potential for rapid growth. The initial staff numbers tend to be low, but the vast majority of the staff will provide either highly skilled or very specific skills. One of the key features of start-ups is prompt adaptation to developing market trends with scope for rapid expansion.

Graduates with business and economic degrees may either be involved in founding start-ups or become involved at an early stage in the life of a company. The disadvantages of start-ups are fairly clear: long hours and low job security, but there are significant potential advantages beyond the obvious possibility of considerable financial reward if the company has identified and exploited the proverbial 'gap in the market'. Start-up companies offer young graduates the chance to enjoy a measure of autonomy not usually available, or at least immediately available, in larger, more heavily structured companies. Also, you may be interested in business, finance and economic developments, but you do not view yourself as a 'corporate' individual. Start-ups generally offer a more relaxed, less regimented power structure, enabling you to input ideas into the company in a more receptive environment. The website Startups would be a good place to begin, especially www.startups. co.uk/guides. Also, start-up companies might be more receptive to potential internships or work experience applications if you can offer the company some relevant previous experience or expertise.

Transport management

Some of the world's biggest businesses are involved in the movement of people and goods, and transport managers are responsible for the safety and efficiency of passenger or freight services. This might include managing and administering places such as airports, railway stations, ports and bus or freight depots on a day-to-day basis. Tasks could include scheduling and timetabling. The role of the transport manager also covers finance, marketing and personnel management.

If there is an accident, it is the job of the transport manager to investigate and take any necessary action. A vital task is to ensure that health and safety regulations are enforced. To be successful in transport management you must be good at organising and planning and enjoy working with figures. It is important that you can remain calm under pressure, but are able to think quickly and logically on your feet. Teamwork and good interpersonal skills are essential.

Both business- and management-related degrees would provide the necessary knowledge and skills for a career in transport management. You could also look at more specialised transport management degrees.

Project management

Many firms organise their staff into specific project teams instead of the traditional functions of marketing, finance, personnel and so on. People on a specific project will come from a variety of different business backgrounds and work together for the duration of that project, often as a team, sharing tasks and responsibilities. You could lead the project as project manager, which requires great skill but can also be exhilarating.

Management degrees would be the most suitable for a student aiming at project management as a future career. There are many specialised degree courses available, including building project management, project engineering and even public art project management.

Management consultancy

The International Guide to Management Consultancy: The Evolution, Practice and Structure defines a management consultant as an independent and qualified person who provides a professional service to business, the public and other undertakings. Management consultants identify and investigate problems in a company concerned with strategy, policy, markets, organisation, procedures and methods. Generally, a team is sent to spend time with the organisation to find out what the problems are. It then comes up with a set of recommendations for action by collecting and analysing the facts, still keeping in mind the broader management and business implications.

Finally, it discusses and agrees on the most appropriate courses of action with the client, and may remain at the company for a short period to help implement these strategies.

Management consultants are high-fliers – they can be recruited from the top graduates, but they are usually people with business experience. This is because, if you are going to have any credibility in advising others how to run their businesses, you need real-life understanding of such issues. You will also need to be quite sensitive and tactful and have a good deal of maturity. Excellent numeracy, teamwork and inter-personal skills are all essential, as is a strong academic background (usually meaning at least a 2.i degree from a prestigious university).

Management degrees would provide a good deal of useful background and training for anyone interested in a management consultancy career. Given the need for analytical and numeracy skills, economics graduates would also satisfy this requirement. There are many very specialised management degrees on offer; you can find these using the 'Course Search' facility on the UCAS website.

General management in large companies

Large companies will often have general managers who are responsible for the general running and operational details of a business. Their role is to liaise with other departments, monitor how members of staff are recruited and make sure that training is kept up to date. The general manager is also responsible for ensuring that profit targets are met, as well as keeping an eye on the marketing and promotional aims of the organisation.

Several large businesses run training schemes for both school-leavers and graduates as management trainees. Most schemes provide an initial period of training, often 12 to 18 months, in which you are placed in a number of departments in the organisation, such as finance, sales and marketing. This is a great opportunity to try out different areas and find out what you like and what you are good at – a bit like a Foundation course. At the end of the training period, you can decide where you want to specialise.

A number of companies have fast-track management programmes with accelerated training and early responsibility. Many university manage-ment departments will have close links with large companies to provide internships, training or to arrange sandwich-year placements.

Management in small businesses

Large company management training schemes, especially with blue chip organisations, are always going to be the most competitive to get on to. You will certainly get a good and thoroughly structured training from them, but you should not overlook the often excellent experience you can gain from a smaller organisation.

In a smaller organisation, you will probably be thrown in at the deep end and are unlikely to have very specific responsibilities, but you will see at close hand the prizes and pitfalls of a career in business. You will also see demonstrated the difference effective marketing can make, and gain first-hand experience of things such as dealing with banks and coping with disgruntled customers – in other words, the reality of working in business.

Managing a small business requires practical skills as well as an understanding of theory. Most business degrees will focus on these skills.

Entrepreneurship

If you have a good idea, have some experience of constructing cash-flow forecasts and are not afraid of failure or hard work, setting up your own company could be your route into the world of business. Richard Branson started his business empire while still at school, as did Alan Sugar. Other useful role models might include the entrepreneurs James Dyson (founder of technology company Dyson Ltd) or Ade Hassan (founder of beauty product company Nubian Skin).

However, it is more common for someone to set up on their own after gaining experience in another organisation. If you are thinking of starting your own business, you will need a lot of the skills and business awareness that are best gained from employment. Added to which, you will need to be innovative and creative, energetic and resilient, persistent and prepared to work long hours. You will need to be realistic in your business plans, and able to adapt rapidly to changing circumstances. It can be very fulfilling to be self-employed, but make sure it is for you before choosing this route.

Successful entrepreneurs tend to be dynamic people with a clear vision of what they want to achieve. Degree courses cannot teach students to be successful entrepreneurs, but a degree in business studies will give a budding entrepreneur the practical skills and knowledge base to supplement his or her ambitions and ideas. There are many degree courses that focus on entrepreneurship, often combined with other disciplines such as mathematics or a language.

Case study

While completing his A levels, Nick worked part time in a high-end jewellery shop. He studied business administration at university and continued working at the jewellers throughout all of his holidays. This gave him an insight into the industry and invaluable contacts which he used to get a work-experience placement at a top auction house in London and later a similar, paid role in New York. Nick now runs his own successful diamond-sourcing business.

'In my mid-twenties when my peers started to get engaged, I realised that I was in a position to help friends get something very unique. That was when I decided to set up my own, bespoke diamond ring business. My background in business was invaluable and I was able to handle the marketing, branding, accounts and operations alone at first. After the company gathered some momentum I began to outsource some of the activity, which gives me support when I need it without the burden of employing full-time staff.'

What makes a good manager?

Many students are attracted by the thought of a managerial career. It has the advantage of being open to graduates from any discipline and work is rewarded on merit – your worth is judged by your performance. A managerial career does not depend on seniority, and it can offer its own rewards, stemming from practical achievement in a job where results can be measured. While a degree in management will not automatically make you a good manager (just as a business studies degree does not necessarily make you a successful businessperson), it does provide you with the academic and practical skills that are necessary for a successful career in management. Bear in mind, however, that there are other ways to acquire these skills.

Different managerial roles require different skills, but a general idea of what companies require of their managers is given in the next section.

Management skills

Managers today have to work in an ever-changing and complex business environment; they need to use an increasing number of analytical methods and techniques. An important skill lies in knowing which techniques to use in a given situation, and how to use them correctly. Here are the main skills you will need to be an effective manager.

Leadership

Good managers are also leaders. The real challenge of management lies in empowering your team to take charge of a project or goal and together achieve more than they believed they could possibly handle. On a management degree course, you would look at different leadership models.

Delegating

Management involves delegating power and responsibility appropriately, not preventing others from developing by hanging on to everything, but equally not giving colleagues unachievable workloads or putting impossible expectations on them.

Getting things done

Good managers are the people who get things done, and they do this by inspiring and encouraging the people working with them.

Teamwork

Teamwork plays a huge part in successful management and is the main reason why employers frequently ask candidates about their extra-curricular achievements and activities. Playing a sport, taking part in dramatic productions or being involved in a school magazine or university society all show an ability to work in a team.

Managing your own work

It is essential that the good manager is effective at managing their own workload well and setting standards for their team. This means setting an example in areas such as good organisation, timekeeping, commitment, personal presentation and honesty.

Managing stress

Because of the pressures of management, good managers will do whatever they can to avoid the effects of undue stress on their physical and mental health – and therefore their productivity. This means having problem-solving skills: you will need to notice if a stressful situation is developing and affecting a team or its members, and be able to deal with it successfully.

Political awareness

Every organisation has its own culture and politics. Good managers will be aware of the context in which they work, including the sensitivities of other people and other departments, so that they can be most effective at motivating their teams.

Managing functions

The management role is broad ranging, and responsibilities can be spread over several business areas or functions. For example:

- operations: maintaining and improving delivery of the service or product for which they are responsible
- finance: budgeting and monitoring the use of resources
- people: motivating those they work with
- information: communicating effectively with everyone at all levels.

Languages

Language skills are essential, and already more than half of the world's population speaks a second language. To enable effective communication with others, you need to cope with the nuances of speech as well as understanding documents such as letters and reports. If you are an English speaker you can get by in Scandinavia, the Netherlands, Germany, much of Central and Eastern Europe and sometimes in France and Belgium without local language skills. (This would not, perhaps, be so easy in Spain or Italy.) But in any situation, you will always be at an advantage if you are able to hold at least a simple conversation in the language of the country in which you are working.

11 | Further information

Useful addresses

ACCA UK
The Adelphi
1–11 John Adam Street
London WC2N 6AU
Tel: 0141 582 2000 (ACCA Connect)
Fax: 020 7059 5050
Email: info@accaglobal.com
Web: www.accaglobal.com

British Chambers of Commerce
65 Petty France
London SW1H 9EU
Tel: 020 7654 5800
Web: www.britishchambers.org.uk

Chartered Governance Institute
Saffron House
6–10 Kirby Street
London EC1N 8TS
Tel: 020 7580 4741
Web: www.cgi.org.uk

Chartered Institute of Credit Management
1 Accent Park
Bakewell Road
Orton Southgate
Peterborough PE2 6XS
Tel: 01780 722900
Web: www.cicm.com

Chartered Institute of Logistics and Transport
Earlstrees Court
Earlstrees Road
Corby NN17 4AX
Tel: 01536 740100
Web: www.ciltuk.org.uk

Chartered Institute of Management Accountants
The Helicon
One South Place
London EC2M 2RB
Tel: 020 8849 2251
Web: www.cimaglobal.com

Chartered Institute of Marketing
Moor Hall
Cookham
Maidenhead SL6 9QH
Tel: 01628 427120
Web: www.cim.co.uk

Chartered Institute of Personnel and Development
151 The Broadway
London SW19 1JQ
Tel: 020 8612 6200
Web: www.cipd.co.uk

Chartered Institute of Purchasing and Supply
Easton House
Church Street
Easton on the Hill
Stamford PE9 3NZ
Tel: 01780 756777
Web: www.cips.org

Chartered Management Institute
Management House
Cottingham Road
Corby NN17 1TT
Tel: 01536 204222
Web: www.managers.org.uk

Chartered Quality Institute
2nd Floor North
Chancery Exchange
10 Furnival Street
London EC4A 1AB
Tel: 020 7245 6722
Web: www.quality.org

Confederation of British Industry
Cannon Place
78 Cannon Street
London EC4N 6HN
Tel : 020 7379 7400
Web: www.cbi.org.uk

Department for Communities
Lighthouse Building
1 Cromac Place
Gasworks Business Park
Ormeau Road
Belfast BT7 2JB
Tel: 028 9082 9000
Web: www.communities-ni.gov.uk

Department for the Economy
Netherleigh
Massey Avenue
Belfast BT4 2JP
Tel: 028 9052 9900
Web: www.economy-ni.gov.uk

Federation of Small Businesses
Sir Frank Whittle Way
Blackpool FY4 2FE
Tel: 0808 20 20 888
Web: www.fsb.org.uk

Higher Education Funding Council for Wales
Tŷ Aron
Bedwas Road
Bedwas
Caerphilly CF83 8WT
Tel: 029 2085 9696
Web: www.hefcw.ac.uk

Institute of Administrative Management
Coppice House
Halesfield 7
Telford TF7 4NA
Tel: 01952 797396
Web: www.instam.org

Institute of Directors
116 Pall Mall
London SW1Y 5ED
Tel: 020 7766 8866
Web: www.iod.com

Institute of Management Services
Brooke House
24 Dam Street
Lichfield WS13 6AA
Tel: 01543 266909
Web: www.ims-productivity.com

Institute of Materials, Minerals and Mining
1 Carlton House Terrace
London SW1Y 5DB
Tel: 020 7451 7300
Web: www.iom3.org

Logistics UK
Hermes House
St John's Road
Tunbridge Wells TN4 9UZ
Tel: 03717 112222
Web: www.logitics.org.uk

Management Consultancies Association
5th Floor
36–38 Cornhill
London EC3V 3NG
Tel: 020 7645 7950
Web: www.mca.org.uk

Operational Research Society
Seymour House
12 Edward Street
Birmingham B1 2RX
Tel: 0121 233 9300
Web: www.theorsociety.com

Prince's Trust
18 Park Square East
London NW1 4LH
Tel: 020 7543 1234
Web: www.princes-trust.org.uk

Scottish Funding Council
Donaldson House
97 Haymarket Terrace
Edinburgh EH12 5HD
Tel: 0131 313 6500
Web: www.sfc.ac.uk

Work Foundation
1 Northumberland Avenue
Trafalgar Square
London WC2N 5BW
Tel: 0207 872 5416

Books

General higher education

Getting into Oxford & Cambridge 2024 Entry, 26th edition, Matthew Carmody, Trotman Education

HEAP 2024: University Degree Course Offers, 54th edition, Brian Heap, Trotman Education

How to Complete Your UCAS Application 2024 Entry, 35th edition, Duncan Chamberlain & UCAS, Trotman Education

Business, economics and management

Bounce: The Myth of Talent and the Power of Practice, M. Syed, HarperCollins

Business Stripped Bare: Adventures of a Global Entrepreneur, Sir R. Branson, Virgin Books

Business: The Ultimate Resource, C. Bartlett, M. Belbin & W. Bennis, A & C Black

Capital in the Twenty-First Century, T. Piketty, Harvard University Press

Cityboy: Beer and Loathing in the Square Mile, G. Anderson, Headline

The Credit Crunch: Housing Bubbles, Globalisation and the Worldwide Economic Crisis, G. Turner, Pluto Press

Economics for Business and Management, A. Griffiths & S. Wall, Pearson Education

Effective Small Business Management, N.M. Scarborough, Pearson Education

The Essential Drucker: The Best of Sixty Years of Peter Drucker's Essential Writings on Management, P. Drucker, HarperCollins

Essential Manager's Manual, R. Heller & T. Hindle, Dorling Kindersley

Freakonomics: A Rogue Economist Explores the Hidden Side of Everything, S.D. Levitt & S.J. Dubner, Penguin

How I Caused the Credit Crunch, T. Ishikawa, Icon Books

How Markets Fail: The Logic of Economic Calamities, J. Cassidy, Penguin

Human Resource Management: A Contemporary Approach, J. Beardwell & T. Claydon, Pearson Education

Iconoclast: A Neuroscientist Reveals How to Think Differently, G. Berns, Harvard Business School Press

Innovation and Entrepreneurship, P.F. Drucker, Butterworth Heinemann

A Little History of Economics, N. Kishtainy, Yale University Press

The New Pioneers: Sustainable Business Success Through Social Innovation and Social Entrepreneurship, T. Ellis, John Wiley & Sons

No Logo, N. Klein, Fourth Estate

The Real Deal: My Story from Brick Lane to Dragons' Den, J. Caan, Virgin Books

Reinventing Management: Smarter Choices for Getting Work Done, J. Birkinshaw, John Wiley & Sons

The Shock Doctrine: The Rise of Disaster Capitalism, N. Klein, Penguin

The Snowball: Warren Buffett and the Business of Life, A. Schroeder, Bloomsbury

Superfreakonomics: Global Cooling, Patriotic Prostitutes and Why Suicide Bombers Should Buy Life Insurance, S.D. Levitt & S.J. Dubner, Penguin

Thinking Fast and Slow, D. Kahneman, Penguin

The Undercover Economist, T. Harford, Abacus

What They Teach You at Harvard Business School: My Two Years Inside the Cauldron of Capitalism, P. Delves Broughton, Penguin

Whoops!: Why Everyone Owes Everyone and No One Can Pay, J. Lanchester, Penguin

Useful websites

Business and financial news

www.bbc.co.uk/news
www.businessweek.com
www.economist.com
www.ft.com
www.telegraph.co.uk/business

Financial organisations

www.wto.org
www.worldbank.org

University entrance

www.ucas.com
www.guardian.co.uk/education/universityguide

Glossary

Administration
A process which allows struggling companies to attempt a comeback by allowing them to continue to operate under close supervision. Companies in administration need permission from a court before they can be dissolved.

Austerity
A policy implemented by government to reduce deficit. This will involve spending cuts, which often means a reduction in benefits and public services. It may also mean increases in taxation.

Bailout
The provision of financial assistance to a government or business in order to prevent the consequences that would arise from its financial collapse. This may be provided in the form of a loan, stocks, cash, bonds or guaranteeing of assets/debts. A bailout may come with terms attached and may or may not have to be repaid.

Balance of trade
The difference between a country's earnings from exports and the amount it spends on imports.

BRICS
Brazil, Russia, India, China and South Africa. Sometimes referred to as the 'Big Five', the economies of these developing countries are growing very fast.

Clearing
A UCAS system that allows students who are not holding any offers to try to get a place on a course with remaining vacancies. If you get higher grades than predicted and decide to reject your firm unconditional choice you can release yourself into Clearing.

Clearing Plus
A UCAS system for candidates who were unsuccessful with their application or are applying for the first time using Clearing. You'll be able to 'view your matches' in your UCAS Hub, which will show a personalised list of courses that are likely to accept you. These 'matches' are what UCAS have found for you based on the information you provided in your application.

Common market
A group of countries that have agreed to promote duty-free trade and free movement of labour between members. They also agree to set common tariffs for imports coming from outside member countries. The European community is a good example of this.

Confederation of British Industry (CBI)
A lobbying organisation that looks after the interests of British businesses at home and overseas. By working with government bodies and legislators it seeks to promote conditions in which British business can compete and thrive.

Credit crunch
A condition where borrowing is difficult because of fears about the ability of borrowers to repay loans. A shrinking credit supply will slow economic growth and it becomes more difficult for borrowers to repay existing debts.

Default
The failure to meet the terms of a loan or another debt.

Deficit
A shortfall in revenue. A government budget deficit describes a situation where the amount a government spends is greater than its income.

Deflation
Negative inflation, where the prices of commodities and services drop on average across the economy.

Double-dip recession
A secondary recession following a brief recovery from a previous period of negative growth.

ECB
The European Central Bank, responsible for monetary policy in the Eurozone. Specifically it aims to keep inflation low and prevent deflation.

Eurozone
An economic and monetary union of the 19 countries which use the euro as their common currency.

Extra
A UCAS process that allows you to add one extra choice at a time (between February and July) if you are holding no offers.

GDP
Gross domestic product. The market value of goods and services produced within a country during a one-year period (plus the value of exports minus the value of imports). It is an indicator of economic activity for a country during a specified period.

Hub
A UCAS online applications system that you use to register and apply to your university choices. You can sign in to your Hub to check your application's progress at any time, including any interview invitations and offers you receive. On results day, you will need to use the UCAS Hub system to track your applications, manage offers and go through Clearing if needed.

IELTS

The International English Language Testing System is a standardised test of proficiency in the English language and is widely accepted by British universities.

IMF

The International Monetary Fund. An organisation set up after World War II to provide financial assistance to governments. The IMF has provided rescue loans to developing countries with debt issues, and more recently has been involved in bailouts for EU governments during the European debt crisis.

Inflation

An increase in prices of goods and services in an economy over a period of time.

Macroeconomics

The study of economic issues across a whole economy. It looks at economy-wide patterns in areas such as trade.

Microeconomics

The study of choices made by individuals and businesses in order to better understand behaviour. Microeconomists often use this sort of information to understand supply and demand in particular markets (e.g. oil or coffee) and to make predictions about how markets will react to external influences.

OPEC

The Organization of Petroleum Exporting Countries. It currently consists of 13 countries: Algeria, Angola, Congo, Equatorial Guinea, Gabon, Iran, Iraq, Kuwait, Libya, Nigeria, Saudi Arabia, the United Arab Emirates and Venezuela.

Personal statement

This is where you have 47 lines (or 4,000 characters including spaces, whichever you use first) to convince the five universities you are applying to that you are right for the course.

Recession

A slowdown in economic activity. A country is technically in recession following two consecutive periods of negative growth.

UCAS

Universities and Colleges Admissions Service. You need to apply to UCAS by the appropriate closing date (see www.ucas.com for more details). You can apply for up to five choices for all courses except medicine, dentistry and veterinary science/medicine (which are limited to a maximum of four choices, although you can make another subject your fifth choice).